COMMON CORE STANDARDS

for | High School
English Language Arts

Edited by John Kendall

COMMON CORE STANDARDS

for High School
English Language Arts

Susan Ryan

Dana Frazee

Alexandria, Virginia USA

Mid-continent Research for Education and Learning
Denver, Colorado USA

1703 N. Beauregard St. • Alexandria, VA 22311-1714 USA
Phone: 800-933-2723 or 703-578-9600 • Fax: 703-575-5400
Website: www.ascd.org • E-mail: member@ascd.org
Author guidelines: www.ascd.org/write

MCREL

Mid-continent Research for Education and Learning
4601 DTC Boulevard, Suite 500
Denver, CO 80237 USA
Phone: 303-337-0990 • Fax: 303-337-3005
Website: www.mcrel.org • E-mail: info@mcrel.org

PAPERBACK ISBN: 978-1-4166-1461-6   ASCD product #113010   n10/12

Also available as an e-book (see Books in Print for the ISBNs).

Quantity discounts: 10–49 copies, 10%; 50+ copies, 15%; for 1,000 or more copies, call 800-933-2723, ext. 5634, or 703-575-5634. For desk copies: www.ascd.org/deskcopy.

Library of Congress Cataloging-in-Publication Data
Ryan, Susan.
  Common core standards for high school English language arts : a quick-start guide / Susan Ryan and Dana Frazee.
      pages cm
  Includes bibliographical references.
  ISBN 978-1-4166-1461-6 (pbk. : alk. paper) 1. Language arts (Secondary)—United States. 2. Language arts (Secondary)—Standards—United States. I. Title.
  LB1631.R94 2012
  428.0071'2–dc23
                                                              2012033783

22 21 20 19 18 17 16 15 14 13 12   1 2 3 4 5 6 7 8 9 10 11 12

COMMON CORE STANDARDS

for | High School
English Language Arts

Acknowledgments

We would like to acknowledge Kirsten Miller and John Kendall for their crucial role in making our thoughts much more readable; Greg Gallagher and the North Dakota Curriculum Initiative committee, who provided us with valuable insights into the challenges facing teachers as they begin to work with the Common Core standards; Ceri Dean for her step-by-step guide to lesson planning; Kathy Olson for her collaboration and content expertise in developing the lessons; our McREL colleagues, who provided an analytical ear as we discussed the work; and our families, for supporting us as we worked on this project.

Introduction

In July 2009, nearly all state school superintendents and the nation's governors joined in an effort to identify a common set of standards in mathematics and English language arts (ELA), with the goal of providing a clear, shared set of expectations that would prepare students for success in both college and career. The Common Core State Standards Initiative (CCSSI) brought together researchers, academics, teachers, and others who routed multiple drafts of the standards to representatives including curriculum directors, content specialists, and technical advisors from all participating state departments of education. By spring 2010, drafts were submitted for comment to the national subject-area organizations and posted for public comment. In June 2010, the final versions were posted to a dedicated website: www.corestandards.org. (A minor update of the standards was posted in October 2010.)

At press time, 46 states, as well as Washington, D.C., and two territories, have adopted the Common Core State Standards (CCSS) for English language arts. (Minnesota has adopted the ELA standards but not the mathematics standards. Texas, Alaska, Virginia, and Nebraska have indicated that they do not plan to adopt either set, although both Virginia and Nebraska have aligned the Common Core standards with their existing standards.)

Adoption of the standards is, of course, voluntary for states and does not include a commitment to any other programs or policies. However, states that have adopted these standards will be eligible to join one of two federally funded assessment consortia that are currently tasked with developing assessments for the Common Core—the Smarter Balanced Assessment Consortium (SBAC) or the Partnership for Assessment of Readiness for College and Careers (PARCC). Sharing assessments across states promises financial relief from notoriously expensive state assessments. In addition, federal programs such as Race to the Top have required that applicants demonstrate that they have joined with other states in adopting a common set of standards and an assessment program. Although states may form new consortia, many either have opted to join or are considering joining SBAC or PARCC.

Sharing a set of standards across states offers other advantages. For example, teachers' well-designed lesson plans targeting Common Core standards will be immediately useful to a large number of colleagues. The shared language of standards should also provide teachers with more opportunities to participate in very specific discussions about content, a process that has been hampered somewhat by the variety of ways states have described virtually the same content.

For a lengthier discussion of the Common Core standards, including their link to previous standards-based education efforts and the benefits and challenges the Common Core presents, see *Understanding Common Core State Standards* (Kendall, 2011), the first booklet in this series. We also encourage readers to explore numerous resources available at corestandards.org, especially the standards document itself (CCSSI, 2010c), the document's appendixes (CCSSI, 2010d, 2010e, 2010f), and the guidelines for adapting standards instruction for English language learners (CCSSI, 2010a) and students with disabilities (CCSSI, 2010b).

About This Guide

This guide is part of a series intended to further the discussion and under-standing of Common Core standards on a subject-specific and grade-level basis and to provide immediate guidance to teachers who must either adapt existing lessons and activities to incorporate the Common Core or develop new lessons to address concepts not addressed in their previous state standards.

After an overview of the structure of the ELA standards, we examine the high school standards in depth, describing how they are designed to help students build upon and extend skills and knowledge acquired in ear-lier grades. Next, we focus on practical lesson planning with the Common Core, looking at a process for creating standards-based lessons that make the best use of the effective instructional strategies explored in *Classroom Instruction That Works, 2nd edition* (Dean, Hubbell, Pitler, & Stone, 2012). The guide concludes with an illustration of this process's outcome: three sample lessons that address Common Core standards identified as repre-senting notable changes to teachers' current practice.

CHAPTER 1

About the Common Core English Language Arts Standards for High School

This chapter focuses on key areas of the Common Core standards for English language arts that represent the most significant changes to commonly used curricula and presents an overview of how the standards are organized, fit together, and reinforce one another. Reviewing the essential student knowledge and skills in the Common Core will allow teachers to quickly understand how they might adjust the materials and strategies used in their classroom to best meet these new expectations.

Focus Areas and Instructional Implications

Although the Common Core ELA standards are comprehensive and address a broad range of communication skills, they place particular emphasis on five key areas: reading informational text, reading complex text, close reading and citing text evidence, writing arguments, and research. Let's take a closer look at each area and consider its implications for teachers.

Reading informational text

During the last decade, the amount of nonfiction included in literature textbooks and on national reading tests such as the National Assessment of Educational Progress (NAEP) has been increasing. The Common Core standards add momentum to this trend, calling for a balance between literature and informational texts in the curriculum. The standards also emphasize domain-specific vocabulary and informative writing, requiring that students read texts that provide rich subject-area content and models of expository structures. For high school English language arts teachers, this shift means that they will need to incorporate more literary nonfiction into their classrooms, giving students the opportunity to read and build knowledge about a wide variety of subjects through nonfiction texts geared toward a general audience.

Reading complex text

The Common Core defines a three-part model for selecting texts in each grade span that will lead to college and career readiness by the end of high school. Within this model, text readability—specifically, its quantitative measure for relative difficulty—is set higher than the mark established by prior readability systems and reading comprehension assessments. This change will have a strong impact on which texts, and in particular which informational texts, are appropriate for high school students. The qualitative measures and reader task considerations, which are the other two legs in the model for text selection in the Common Core, provide teachers with a set of criteria to use when evaluating titles appropriate for students. The particular challenge for high school English teachers may be ensuring that the texts students read build steadily in complexity over the sequence of traditional high school courses, from World Literature to American Literature to British Literature.

Close reading and citing text evidence

The Common Core has numerous reading standards that ask students to closely analyze the information, ideas, and rhetorical choices that appear in texts. Students are expected to provide text evidence to support their assertions about the content and rhetoric in texts that they read. Teachers may emphasize this type of close reading and use of text evidence in their classrooms by increasing the number of text-based questions that they ask. Currently, many questions in the curriculum are designed to develop student background knowledge or to help students make connections between the text and their prior experience. The Common Core publishers' criteria document (Coleman & Pimentel, 2012) estimates that in order to match the requirements of the reading standards, 80 to 90 percent of questions teachers ask should be text-based. It's also recommended that teachers increase their use of graphic organizers and activities that ask students to provide direct quotations from the text as evidence. Teachers will need to inventory and review their current curriculum, identifying the types of questions and organizers they use so that they may make plans for modification.

Writing arguments

The Common Core includes many standards that ask students to evaluate and develop formal, logical arguments based on text evidence. While prior state standards typically described a broad set of skills related to persuasion, they did not place particular emphasis on dissecting logical arguments. Teachers will need to incorporate lessons that ask students to analyze exemplar arguments, as well as increase the number of writing and speaking assignments in which students argue their opinion about a topic or theme, using text-based evidence as support.

Research

The research standards in the Common Core are not a significant departure from those found in most state standards, and most teachers may find that they are accustomed to covering similar content during the course of a year. However, the Common Core specifies that students conduct both brief and sustained research and that this research be woven into many different classroom contexts. Likewise, standards throughout the Common Core reflect research skills requiring students to compare and integrate information from diverse sources. Teachers seeking to implement the Common Core standards will likely need to increase the number of activities in which students gather and synthesize information.

How the Standards Are Organized

The Common Core ELA standards present content within a highly organized structure, first by strands and then by more specific headings. The standards themselves provide the most detailed level of content description: statements of student knowledge and skills for particular grades. For high school students, standards are divided into two grade bands, 9–10 and 11–12. Each grade-level content standard can be traced back to the Common Core's foundation: the set of College and Career Readiness anchor standards (CCRA) that broadly describe what students should know and be able to do by the time they graduate high school. To further clarify the structure of the Common Core standards, we will look at each organizational component in turn.

Strands

The ELA standards are sorted into four strands: Reading, Writing, Speaking and Listening, and Language. The first three of these categories will be familiar, as they have been used to organize content in numerous state ELA standards documents. The category of Language, however, is found less frequently in state standards. The Common Core Language strand describes skills that may be applied to one or more of the other strands. For example, grammar may be applied to both writing and speaking activities, and vocabulary is an important element of reading, writing, speaking, and listening. The strands are also distinguished from some state standards in that research skills and media literacy are not separate categories; research is addressed in the Common Core Writing strand, and media is embedded throughout the ELA strands, with some emphasis in the Speaking and Listening strand. At the middle school and high school levels, the Reading strand is further subdivided into two domains: the Reading Standards for Literature and the Reading Standards for Informational Text. The standards in these two domains are parallel, addressing the same basic reading skills but describing them in ways specific to reading fiction versus reading literary nonfiction.

Each strand has an associated abbreviation code to identify its particular numbered standards, with each of the two domains of the Reading strand receiving its own shorthand:

- Reading Literature (RL)
- Reading Informational Text (RI)
- Writing (W)
- Speaking and Listening (SL)
- Language (L)

These strand abbreviations are used as part of the CCSSI's official identification system, which provides a unique identifier for each standard in the Common Core and can be very useful to school staffs developing crosswalks, planning lessons, and sharing lesson plans. For example, the sixth standard in the Writing strand can be referred to as "Writing Standard 6" or, using the full, formal "dot notation," as "CCSS.ELA-Literacy.W.6." To speak specifically of a standard for a particular high school grade band, the grade designation is inserted between the strand letter and standard number: "CCSS.ELA-Literacy.W.9–10.6," for example, is Writing Standard 6 for grades 9–10. In this guide, we use an abbreviated form of this identification system, dropping the common prefix and using strand and standard number (e.g., W.6.). In the sample lessons, we insert the grade band indicator.

Headings

Within each strand, a set of two or more topic headings provides further organization. The same headings span all grade levels. In the Language strand, for example, the standards are organized under three headings: Conventions of Standard English, Knowledge of Language, and Vocabulary Acquisition and Use. The headings provide users with an overview of the topics that the particular strands address, group standards that share a similar focus, and provide context for understanding individual standards. For example, the Craft and Structure heading in the Reading strand signals that the standards listed under it will focus on the various choices that authors make when developing (crafting) and organizing (structuring) their writing.

College and Career Readiness Anchor standards

As noted, the College and Career Readiness Anchor standards define the knowledge and skills students should acquire in each content strand over the course of their K–12 education. The more specific, grade-level content standard statements spell out the aspects of CCRA knowledge and skills appropriate for students within each grade band. In other words, there is a version of every anchor standard for each grade level, and every grade level has the same anchor standards. For illustration, see Figure 1.1, which displays the grade-level versions of the same anchor standard within the Reading strand.

In this way, the anchor standards provide overarching goals for student learning. When a single standard includes many details and various aspects, teachers can identify that standard's primary focus by reviewing its associated anchor standard. The progression of grade-level standards

Figure 1.1 **High School Grade-Specific Versions of a CCRA Standard**		
CCRA:	Grades 9–10 Students:	Grades 11–12 Students:
RL.2 Determine central ideas or themes of a text and analyze their development; summarize the key supporting details and ideas.	**RL.9–10.2** Determine a theme or central idea of a text and analyze in detail its development over the course of the text, including how it emerges and is shaped and refined by specific details; provide an objective summary of the text.	**RL.11–12.2** Determine two or more themes or central ideas of a text and analyze their development over the course of the text, including how they interact and build on one another to produce a complex account; provide an objective summary of the text.

provides a structure that indicates how students' skills are expected to advance over time. As teachers assess their students, the continuum of grade-level standards in the Common Core may enhance their understanding of how student skills develop. Additional assistance can be found in a learning progression framework developed by the National Center for the Improvement of Educational Assessment, which identifies research-based learning progressions for use with the Common Core (Hess, 2011).

Connections Across Content Areas

It is important to note that the Common Core ELA standards are published in the same document as the Common Core literacy standards for history/ social studies, science, and technical subjects. Because the literacy standards are intended for teachers in those subject areas, rather than language arts teachers, we do not address them within this guide. However, the Common Core emphasizes an integrated model of literacy that includes cross-subject collaboration among teachers, so language arts teachers will benefit from familiarizing themselves with the literacy standards. Briefly, the literacy standards cover reading and writing and share the same CCRA standards as the ELA standards; the grade-specific literacy standards describe how the same set of skills articulated in the ELA standards should be applied in social studies, science, and technical classrooms.

Appendices to the ELA/Literacy Standards

In addition to the standards themselves, the Common Core standards document for ELA includes a set of three appendices that provide further clarification and support.

Appendix A (CCSSI, 2010d) explains the research base and rationale for many of the key aspects of the standards. It describes how to use the Common Core text complexity model, which includes three factors for determining the appropriate complexity of texts for each grade range. Appendix A also describes the three major text types required by the standards in the Writing strand: argument, exposition, and narration. The role of oral language in literacy is also described, as are various aspects of the Language strand, including vocabulary.

Appendix B (CCSSI, 2010e) provides further support related to text complexity by excerpting portions of particular texts that illustrate the level of complexity required of students within each grade band. Short performance tasks accompany the exemplar texts and indicate the types of activities and student performances that support specific reading standards.

Appendix C (CCSSI, 2010f) provides annotated samples of student writing for each grade level that meet or exceed the minimum level of proficiency the standards demand. Examples are provided across all three of the text types: argument, informational/expository, and narrative writing. In most cases, the samples are accompanied by a description of the context for writing (prompt, requirements, audience, and purpose). Annotations help clarify how the samples meet the requirements of the grade-level standards.

✷✷✷

As noted, our intention in this quick-start guide is to provide a sense of the meaning of each high school ELA standard and explain how the standards are related to each other across grades and strands. Please be aware that what we present are only a few examples of such connections, and we do not mean to suggest that no other connections can or should be made. Teachers should build on the information here to strengthen their own practice and enhance their implementation of the Common Core standards.

Now that we've looked at the overall structure of the Common Core ELA standards, we will examine each strand in turn.

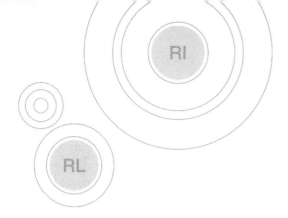

CHAPTER 2

Reading

The Common Core standards expect students to read both widely and deeply. Students read across a variety of genres and time periods to develop cultural appreciation and insights into the human condition. At the same time, they read materials closely, thinking critically about the presented concepts and dissecting the author's execution of his or her craft. As discussed later in this chapter, a key aspect of the standards is that they provide an opportunity for all students to encounter and learn from complex texts that prepare them for the level of reading required in college and careers.

The Reading strand is divided into two domains: the Reading Standards for Literature (the "reading literature" standards or "RL") and the Reading Standards for Informational Text (the "reading informational text" standards or "RI"). Each of these domains shares the same College and Career Readiness anchor standards and the same four headings: Key Ideas and Details, Craft and Structure, Integration of Knowledge and Ideas, and Range of Reading and Level of Text Complexity. The reading literature standards and reading informational text standards share a number of similarities. In this chapter, we'll review both domains, alternating our focus between them as we move from one heading to the next and using excerpts from the Common Core as the basis for discussion.

Key Ideas and Details

Figure 2.1 shows the sequence of the reading literature standards under the Key Ideas and Details heading. Differences in each standard's phrasing from the prior grade level are shown in contrasting text to highlight how the content changes from grade to grade.

Phrased identically in the literature and informational text domains, Reading Standard 1 (abbreviated as RL.1 and RI.1, respectively) provides a foundation for the Common Core focus on students' close, analytic reading and gathering of supporting text evidence. The majority of standards in the Reading strand ask students to analyze or evaluate texts, and this first standard requires them to thoroughly support those analyses with text

RL.1–3

Figure 2.1 ⏐ **Reading Literature Standards 1–3: Key Ideas and Details**	
Grades 9–10 Students:	Grades 11–12 Students:
RL.1 Cite strong **and thorough** textual evidence to support analysis of what the text says explicitly as well as inferences drawn from the text.	**RL.1** Cite strong and thorough textual evidence to support analysis of what the text says explicitly as well as inferences drawn from the text, **including determining where the text leaves matters uncertain.**
RL.2 Determine a theme or central idea of a text and analyze **in detail** its development over the course of the text, including **how it emerges and is shaped and refined by specific details;** provide an objective summary of the text.	**RL.2** Determine **two or more** themes or central ideas of a text and analyze their development over the course of the text, including **how they interact and build on one another to produce a complex account;** provide an objective summary of the text.
RL.3 Analyze **how complex characters (e.g., those with multiple or conflicting motivations) develop over the course of a text, interact with other characters, and advance the plot or develop the theme.**	**RL.3** Analyze the **impact of the author's choices regarding how to develop and relate elements of a story or drama (e.g., where a story is set, how the action is ordered, how the characters are introduced and developed).**
Note: Boldface text identifies content that differs from the prior grade level.	

evidence. In this way, it works in tandem with many of the other standards that follow. Across grades, Reading Literature Standard 1 also requires students to comprehend texts and make inferences when reading. In addition, 11th and 12th graders are asked to be aware of instances in which a text is ambiguous; they need to understand when their inferences are not explicitly supported in the text.

Writers of the Common Core note that the standards ask students to "read like a detective" (Coleman & Pimentel, 2012, p. 16), carefully scrutinizing the content, structure, and rhetoric in texts. The next two standards under this heading describe the ways in which students are expected to closely analyze written content, including its key ideas and details.

Reading Literature Standard 2 (RL.2) focuses on determining the main idea or theme and identifying how it is developed through details in the text. The only difference between RL.2 and its counterpart in the reading informational text standards (RI.2) is the inclusion of "themes" in addition to "main ideas."

As they do with all skills addressed in the ELA standards, students build facility with text analysis over the course of their K–12 education. They begin in their elementary years by summarizing main ideas and details gleaned from reading. In high school, their text analysis becomes more sophisticated as they gain a greater understanding of how the presentation of themes and ideas is affected by specific details the author has chosen. For this second reading standard, the skills of students in grades 11–12 have progressed to the point where they are expected to analyze two or more themes or central ideas and explore how details interact with and build on one another to describe complex layers of meaning.

Across all grades, the third standard under the Key Ideas and Details heading, Reading Literature Standard 3, focuses on the interaction and development of individuals, events, and ideas within a text. This standard differs significantly from grade to grade and between its iterations in the Reading strand's two domains.

Within the set of literature standards, RL.3's focus for grades 9–10 is character development. Students have built an understanding of characters in previous grades; in grades 6–8, for example, they investigated the relation-ship between characters and other story elements such as plot and setting. However, as students enter high school, the characters in grade-appropriate works of fiction are becoming more complex, exhibiting multifaceted moti-vations and personalities, and RL.3 reflects this growing complexity. For grades 11–12, RL.3 asks students to consider all narrative elements (setting, plot, characters) and examine how authors develop and orchestrate these elements to create meaning.

Figure 2.2 shows the full sequence of standards under the Key Ideas and Details heading of the Reading Standards for Informational Text.

RI.1–3

Figure 2.2 ǀ **Reading Informational Text Standards 1–3: Key Ideas and Details**	
Grades 9–10 Students:	Grades 11–12 Students:
RI.1 Cite strong **and thorough** textual evidence to support analysis of what the text says explicitly as well as inferences drawn from the text.	**RI.1** Cite strong and thorough textual evidence to support analysis of what the text says explicitly as well as inferences drawn from the text, **including deter-mining where the text leaves matters uncertain.**
RI.2 Determine a central idea of a text and analyze its development over the course of the text, **including how it emerges and is shaped and refined by** specific details; provide an objective summary of the text.	**RI.2** Determine **two or more** central ideas of a text and analyze their develop-ment over the course of the text, includ-ing **how they interact and build on one another to provide a complex analysis;** provide an objective summary of the text.
RI.3 Analyze how **the author unfolds an analysis or series of ideas or events, including the order in which the points are made, how they are introduced and developed, and the connections that are drawn between them.**	**RI.3** Analyze **a complex set of ideas or sequence of events and explain how specific individuals, ideas, or events interact and develop over the course of the text.**

Note: Boldface text identifies content that differs from the prior grade level.

As previously noted, the first two standards are identical, or nearly identical, to the versions in the reading literature domain, addressing textual evidence and analyzing main ideas and details, respectively. Reading Informational Text Standard 3 (RI.3), however, includes more variation in detail and phrasing at each grade. In grades 9–10, students analyze the ideas or events in literary nonfiction in order to understand how authors structure and describe information.

For a lesson addressing Reading Informational Text Standard 3 at the grades 11–12 level (RI.11–12.3), see **Sample Lesson 3.**

Studying techniques that authors of expository texts use to guide readers and make connections among ideas helps students dissect the text's information and may also provide them with models for their own writing. In grades 11–12, RI.3 asks students to continue to analyze how authors effectively convey information as that information increases in complexity.

The standards listed under Key Ideas and Details all relate to comprehending and citing the main ideas and supporting details in texts and to analyzing how those ideas and details relate to one another and accomplish the author's purposes. As with all of the reading standards, the increased level of difficulty from one grade to the next is directly related to the increasing complexity of the text being analyzed, an aspect that is described in detail within the discussion of the Range of Reading and Level of Text Complexity heading (see p. 24).

Notably, the reading standards do not specify the use of particular reading comprehension strategies (such as making predictions), as is common in many state standards documents. The Common Core publishers' criteria document states that, in ELA and literacy, "To be effective, instruction on specific reading techniques should occur when they illuminate specific aspects of a text. Students need to build an infrastructure of skills, habits, knowledge, dispositions, and experience that enables them to approach new challenging texts with confidence and stamina. As much as possible, this training should be embedded in the activity of reading the text rather than [be] taught as a separate body of material" (Coleman & Pimentel, 2012, p. 9). Thus, reading strategies are left to classroom teachers to model and incorporate into instruction as driven by curricula and student needs.

Craft and Structure

The three standards under the Craft and Structure heading require students to evaluate the techniques and strategies that authors employ in texts, analyzing diction, organization, and point of view or purpose. Figure 2.3 shows the sequence of these standards in the reading literature domain.

The first standard, Reading Literature Standard 4 (RL.4), focuses on diction. Students study the explicit and implied meaning of words and phrases used in a text. In high school, students must not only understand the meaning of particular words but also evaluate the impact of the author's word

 RL.4–6

Figure 2.3 | **Reading Literature Standards 4–6: Craft and Structure**

Grades 9–10 Students:	Grades 11–12 Students:
RL.4 Determine the meaning of words and phrases as they are used in the text, including figurative and connotative meanings; analyze the **cumulative** impact of specific word choices on meaning and tone **(e.g., how the language evokes a sense of time and place; how it sets a formal or informal tone).**	**RL.4** Determine the meaning of words and phrases as they are used in the text, including figurative and connotative meanings; analyze the impact of specific word choices on meaning and tone, **including words with multiple meanings or language that is particularly fresh, engaging, or beautiful. (Include Shakespeare as well as other authors.)**
RL.5 Analyze how an author's choices concerning how to structure a text, order events within it (e.g., parallel plots), and manipulate time (e.g., pacing, flashbacks) create such effects as mystery, tension, or surprise.	**RL.5** Analyze how an author's choices concerning how to structure **specific parts of** a text (e.g., **the choice of where to begin or end a story, the choice to provide a comedic or tragic resolution) contribute to its overall structure and meaning as well as its aesthetic impact.**
RL.6 Analyze **a particular point of view or cultural experience reflected in a work of literature from outside the United States, drawing on a wide reading of world literature.**	**RL.6** Analyze **a case in which grasping point of view requires distinguishing what is directly stated in a text from what is really meant (e.g., satire, sarcasm, irony, or understatement).**

Note: Boldface text identifies content that differs from the prior grade level.

choices on the text's overall tone. This focus on how diction affects a work as a whole sets this standard apart from similar standards listed under the Vocabulary Acquisition and Use heading within the Language strand (see p. 53). By grades 11–12, students study exemplars of literary quality that use language in more complex ways, including words and phrases chosen to create layers of meaning. RL.4 specifies that students read Shakespeare and other well-regarded authors, an indication of the quality of diction that students should be able to evaluate by the end of their high school years.

Reading Literature Standard 5 (RL.5) focuses on the structure and organization of texts. In high school, students are asked to become more aware of the choices that authors make when organizing text. In grades 9–10, students analyze the effects that various plot devices, such as parallel plots and flashbacks, have on the audience. In grades 11–12, students consider how choices about very specific plot points contribute to the piece as a whole.

Reading Literature Standard 6 (RL.6) focuses on point of view and perspective. In grades 9–10, this standard specifies that students study point of view or cultural experiences in works of world literature. In grades 11–12, students analyze point of view in texts with contradictions and subtle meanings.

Figure 2.4 lists the Standards for Reading Informational Text under the Craft and Structure heading. While these standards closely resemble their counterparts for reading literature, they include details specific to reading literary nonfiction.

For grades 9–10, Reading Informational Text Standard 4 (RI.4) differs from RL.4 only in the addition of technical meanings and a provided example, which describes how authors select words and phrases for various nonfiction purposes and audiences. This example implies that students should compare diction across texts. Appendix A of the Common Core standards document notes that students require multiple exposures to targeted vocabulary words in a variety of contexts. Thus, teachers selecting texts for curriculum should consider how multiple texts use the same words or phrases and design lessons or units that compare the effect of those words across a variety of text types. RI.4 for grades 11–12 describes how the concept behind a word or phrase may be developed in a piece of literary nonfiction. Similar

RI.4–6

Figure 2.4 | **Reading Informational Text Standards 4–6: Craft and Structure**	
Grades 9–10 Students:	Grades 11–12 Students:
RI.4 Determine the meaning of words and phrases as they are used in a text, including figurative, connotative, and technical meanings; analyze the **cumulative** impact of specific word choices on meaning and tone **(e.g., how the language of a court opinion differs from that of a newspaper).**	**RI.4** Determine the meaning of words and phrases as they are used in a text, including figurative, connotative, and technical meanings; **analyze how an author uses and refines the meaning of a key term or terms over the course of a text (e.g., how Madison defines *faction* in *Federalist* No. 10).**
RI.5 Analyze in detail **how an author's ideas or claims are developed** and refined by particular sentences, paragraphs, **or larger portions of a text (e.g., a section or chapter).**	**RI.5** Analyze **and evaluate the effectiveness of the structure an author uses in his or her exposition or argument, including whether the structure makes points clear, convincing, and engaging.**
RI.6 Determine an author's point of view or purpose in a text and analyze how an author **uses rhetoric to advance that point of view or purpose.**	**RI.6** Determine an author's point of view or purpose **in a text in which the rhetoric is particularly effective, analyzing how style and content contribute to the power, persuasiveness, or beauty of the text.**

Note: Boldface text identifies content that differs from the prior grade level.

to other reading standards at this grade level, students must consider how specific author choices build meaning in the overall work.

Reading Informational Text Standards 5 and 6 (RI.5 and RI.6) deviate somewhat from RL.5 and RL.6.

RI.5 focuses on the ways an author's ideas are structured in sentences, paragraphs, and sections of nonfiction text. Students build the basis for this understanding in prior grades; by grades 9–10, they are able to evaluate a text's organizational details on multiple levels. In grades 11–12, they evaluate the effectiveness of an author's choices for organizing a text, assessing how well the text's structure supports the author's purposes.

Reading Informational Text Standard 6, the final standard under the Craft and Structure heading, focuses on how authors support their point of view or purpose. RI.6 for grades 9–10 asks students to analyze in particular how rhetorical techniques support an author's point of view; the rhetorical devices might include figurative phrases, organizational structures, and other attributes of a text that are the focus of other standards. Students continue to build this in grades 11–12 by reading literary nonfiction that includes increasingly complex and effective rhetoric.

Integration of Knowledge and Ideas

The Integration of Knowledge and Ideas heading covers standards that focus on students' comparing and synthesizing the ideas and information from different works, including multimedia and artistic mediums. Figure 2.5 shows the sequence of these standards for reading literature.

Figure 2.5 | **Reading Literature Standards 7 and 9: Integration of Knowledge and Ideas**	
Grades 9–10 Students:	Grades 11–12 Students:
RL.7 Analyze **the representation of a subject or a key scene in two different artistic mediums, including what is emphasized or absent in each treatment (e.g., Auden's "Musée des Beaux Arts" and Breughel's** *Landscape with the Fall of Icarus*).	**RL.7** Analyze **multiple interpretations of a story, drama, or poem (e.g., recorded or live production of a play or recorded novel or poetry), evaluating how each version interprets the source text. (Include at least one play by Shakespeare and one play by an American dramatist.)**
RL.8 (Not applicable to literature)	**RL.8** (Not applicable to literature)
RL.9 Analyze how **an author** draws on **and transforms** source material in a specific work **(e.g., how Shakespeare treats a theme or topic from Ovid or the Bible or how a later author draws on a play by Shakespeare).**	**RL.9 Demonstrate knowledge of eighteenth-, nineteenth- and early-twentieth-century foundational works of American literature, including how two or more texts from the same period treat similar themes or topics.**
Note: Boldface text identifies content that differs from the prior grade level.	

Both standards under this heading focus on comparing multiple texts or pieces. The first, Reading Literature Standard 7 (RL.7), asks students in grades 9–10 to analyze the treatment of a subject or the production of a scene in two different media, such as poetry and visual art. Students compare works and evaluate the possible reasons for similarities and differences. Building on this skill in grades 11–12, students analyze two or more versions of the same source text and assess each version in light of the others.

Because the reading literature domain does not include Reading Standard 8, which deals with evaluating arguments, we will skip to Reading Literature Standard 9 (RL.9), in which students analyze themes and topics within a single piece of literature and across multiple texts. Students in grades 9–10 analyze literary allusions and assess how a work transforms and builds on ideas found in earlier works. In grades 11–12, they compare works from the same period in American literature.

Figure 2.6 lists the Integration of Knowledge and Ideas standards in the reading informational text domain. Similar to their counterparts in the literature domain, these standards focus on synthesizing and evaluating information from texts.

Reading Informational Text Standard 7 (RI.7) focuses on comparing works that present information on the same subject or topic in different ways. In grades 9–10, students analyze information from two different media, such as print and multimedia sources, and compare differences in emphasis among multiple documents. Students in grades 11–12 also synthesize information presented in different formats, such as models or graphs, but they do so to address a question or solve a problem. There's a clear connection between these standards and those under the Research to Build and Present Knowledge heading of the Writing strand (see p. 37); students are asked to make connections across multiple sources, just as they do when employing a research process.

Reading Informational Text Standard 8 (RI.8 [which, as noted, has no counterpart in the reading literature domain]) focuses on evaluating logic and reasoning in informational texts. This is a key standard in the Common Core, reflecting its emphasis on students' ability to dissect and develop

Figure 2.6 | **Reading Informational Text Standards 7–9: Integration of Knowledge and Ideas**	
Grades 9–10 Students:	Grades 11–12 Students:
RI.7 Analyze various accounts of a subject told in different mediums (e.g., a person's life story in both print and multimedia), determining which details are emphasized in each account.	**RI.7 Integrate and evaluate multiple sources of information** presented in different media **or formats (e.g., visually, quantitatively) as well as in words in order to address a question or solve a problem.**
RI.8 Delineate and evaluate the argument and specific claims in a text, assessing whether the reasoning is **valid** and the evidence is relevant and sufficient; **identify false statements and fallacious reasoning.**	RI.8 Delineate and evaluate **the reasoning in seminal U.S. texts, including the application of constitutional principles and use of legal reasoning (e.g., in U.S. Supreme Court majority opinions and dissents) and the premises, purposes, and arguments in works of public advocacy (e.g., *The Federalist*, presidential addresses).**
RI.9 Analyze **seminal U.S. documents of historical and literary significance (e.g., Washington's Farewell Address, the Gettysburg Address, Roosevelt's Four Freedoms speech, King's "Letter from Birmingham Jail"), including how they address related themes and concepts.**	RI.9 Analyze **seventeenth-, eighteenth-, and nineteenth-century foundational U.S. documents of historical and literary significance (including the Declaration of Independence, the Preamble to the Constitution, the Bill of Rights, and Lincoln's Second Inaugural Address) for their themes, purposes, and rhetorical features.**

Note: Boldface text identifies content that differs from the prior grade level.

arguments. In high school, building on what they've learned in earlier grades, students learn to assess whether the reasoning in a text is valid by identifying false statements and fallacious logic. RI.8 for grades 11–12 emphasizes the complexity of texts to be evaluated for their reasoning, specifying the assessment of historic and U.S. legal documents.

The final reading informational text standard under the Integration of Knowledge and Ideas heading is similar to its counterpart in the reading

For a lesson addressing Reading Informational Text Standard 9 at the grades 11–12 level (RI.11–12.9), see **Sample Lesson 3.**

literature domain in that students analyze texts with shared themes or topics. Reading Informational Text Standard 9 (RI.9) focuses on students building knowledge of a topic by analyzing texts and making connections to other texts. The requirements for grades 9–10 and grades 11–12 are very similar, asking students to study nonfiction texts important to U.S. literature and history. In grades 11–12, students are required to read three specific documents significant to the founding of the U.S. government and one historic speech. Through this requirement, the Common Core seeks to ensure that students gain an understanding of the common themes and topics in significant bodies of literature that are important in the culture and history of the United States.

Range of Reading and Level of Text Complexity

The final heading within the Reading strand covers just a single standard. Reading Standard 10 (RL.10/RI.10) reflects the idea that reading skills must be applied to texts that increase in complexity each year to ensure that students graduate prepared to read entry-level college texts.

It's important to say a few words here about the Common Core text complexity model, which includes three factors: qualitative measures, quantitative measures, and reader and task considerations. These factors are described in detail in Appendix A (CCSSI, 2010d), with models provided in Appendix B (CCSSI, 2010e).

Quantitative measures are objective and may be evaluated using a readability measure, which calculates text difficulty by examining aspects such as word and sentence length. Six different measures for calculating readability were compared in a recent study (Nelson, Perfetti, Liben, & Liben, 2012), and these measures now share a common scale that aligns to college and career readiness as described in the Common Core. These measures include ATOS®, Degrees of Reading Power®, Flesch Kincaid®, Lexile framework®, Source Rater©, and the Pearson Reading Maturity Metric©. Quantitative readability measures do not address drama and poetry, however, and are less accurate for literature than they are for informational texts.

The other factors in the text complexity model are more subjective. Qualitative factors include aspects of the text, such as levels of meaning, structure, language conventionality and clarity, and knowledge demands. Rubrics have been developed by the Kansas State Department of Education (2011) and the National Center for the Improvement of Educational Assessment (Hess & Hervey, 2011) to assess qualitative factors for literature and informational text. These same groups have developed criteria to aid teachers considering the third component of Common Core text complexity, reader and task. This final aspect of the model takes into account students' individual motivation, knowledge, and experiences, as well as the complexity of the assignment. As more educators work to implement the Common Core standards in the coming years, additional tools to aid teachers in evaluating text complexity and selecting appropriate texts for classroom use will likely be developed.

Within the Reading strand, both the Standards for Reading Literature and the Standards for Reading Informational Text describe text complexity in terms of grade bands. In high school, there are two grade bands: one for grades 9–10 and another designated as grade 11–CCR (college and career ready). Students in the lower grade of the band may need supports, such as guided reading, to read texts at the high end of the grade band. Figure 2.7 shows the Range of Reading and Level of Text Complexity standard (RL.10) for the reading literature domain.

In addition to describing text complexity, RL.10 describes the range of student reading by identifying a variety of genres that students should read, including stories, dramas, and poetry. Stories appropriate to grades 6–12 are further defined as adventure stories, historical fiction, mysteries, myths, science fiction, realistic fiction, allegories, parodies, satire, and graphic novels. Drama includes one-act and multi-act plays in written and oral forms. Poetry includes poems written in narrative, lyrical, and free-verse forms; sonnets; odes; ballads; and epics.

Figure 2.8 shows the reading informational text domain's Range of Reading and Level of Text Complexity standard (RI.10). It mirrors RL.10, using identical phrasing to describe text complexity.

Figure 2.7 | **Reading Literature Standard 10: Range of Reading and Level of Text Complexity**

Grades 9–10 Students:	Grades 11–12 Students:
RL.10 By the end of *grade 9,* read and comprehend literature, including stories, dramas, and poems, in the *grades 9–10* text complexity band proficiently, **with scaffolding as needed at the high end of the range.** By the end of *grade 10,* read and comprehend literature, including stories, dramas, and poems, at the high end of the *grades 9–10* text complexity band independently and proficiently.	**RL.10** By the end of *grade 11,* read and comprehend literature, including stories, dramas, and poems, in the *grades 11– CCR* text complexity band proficiently, with scaffolding as needed at the high end of the range. By the end of *grade 12,* read and comprehend literature, including stories, dramas, and poems, at the high end of the *grades 11–CCR* text complexity band independently and proficiently.

Note: Boldface text identifies content that differs from the prior grade level.

Figure 2.8 | **Reading Informational Text Standard 10: Range of Reading and Level of Text Complexity**

Grades 9–10 Students:	Grades 11–12 Students:
RI.10 By the end of *grade 9,* read and comprehend literary nonfiction in the *grades 9–10* text complexity band proficiently, **with scaffolding as needed at the high end of the range.** By the end of *grade 10,* read and comprehend literary nonfiction at the high end of the *grades 9–10* text complexity band independently and proficiently.	**RI.10** By the end of *grade 11,* read and comprehend literary nonfiction in the *grades 11–CCR* text complexity band proficiently, with scaffolding as needed at the high end of the range. By the end of *grade 12,* read and comprehend literary nonfiction at the high end of the *grades 11–CCR* text complexity band independently and proficiently.

Note: Boldface text identifies content that differs from the prior grade level.

In range of reading, RI.10 defines informational texts for grades 6–12 as literary nonfiction, which includes exposition, argument, and functional text in the form of personal essays; speeches; opinion pieces; essays about art or literature; biographies; memoirs; journalism; and historic, scientific, technical, or economic accounts (including digital sources) written for a broad audience. Although literary nonfiction includes genres that are structured similarly to narratives, such as biographies, the standards emphasize nonfiction that is built on informational text structures, such as essays and speeches. Informational documents that are not designed for a wide audience, such as technical reports, should be taught in other subject-area classrooms using the literacy standards for social studies, science, and technical subjects.

In both domains, Reading Standard 10 has clear implications for curriculum and instruction. It calls for teachers to select a variety of reading materials that encompass both the breadth and the complexity described in the standards. The *PARCC Model Content Frameworks* (Partnership for Assessment of Readiness for College and Careers, 2011) suggests that unit plans include a variety of short texts that complement longer texts. For example, short informational texts might build the background knowledge needed to analyze a historical novel. Short texts also may provide greater opportunity for students to reread, which in turn supports the type of close, analytic examination essential to many of the reading standards. Short, complex texts, or short excerpts from longer texts, may be used to model reading strategies and analytic thinking. The mix of short and longer texts will also provide opportunities for students to engage with texts of varying levels of complexity.

While Reading Standard 10 is clear that all students should build proficiency with grade-level complex texts and topics, students also need opportunities to build fluency and vocabulary with texts that they can comprehend independently. Essentially, the Common Core calls for teachers to use the text complexity model to carefully select reading materials of various lengths, genres, and complexity, which will provide all students with the opportunity to increase their reading ability and prepare for the challenges of college or the workplace.

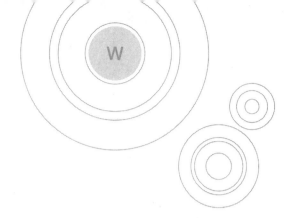

CHAPTER 3

Writing

The Common Core writing standards describe three types of writing: argument, exposition, and narration. They also encompass skills related to writing processes, including using technology and conducting research. Taken together, the standards emphasize writing as a tool that develops students' critical thinking and learning.

The standards in the Writing strand (W) are grouped under four headings: Text Types and Purposes, Production and Distribution of Writing, Research to Build and Present Knowledge, and Range of Writing. Our discussion is organized by heading.

Text Types and Purposes

Across all grades, there are three primary types of writing described under the Text Types and Purposes heading: argumentation, exposition, and narration. For the first two writing types, students write to state an argument or to inform. In both, students support a thesis and develop organized paragraphs based on the content. For the third writing type, narration, students write a story. The Common Core standards call for the same balance of writing types found in the National Assessment of Educational Progress (NAEP). In high school, the allocation is 40 percent argument, 40 percent informative, and 20 percent narrative (National Assessment Governing Board, 2011).

Although the standards describe just three types of writing, they also indicate that as students address specific purposes and audiences, they will employ a wide variety of forms or subgenres, such as speeches, investigative reports, literary analysis, summaries, and research papers.

Appendix A of the standards document notes that effective student writing may blend text types to accomplish a given purpose, such as when an explanatory essay includes a personal anecdote. The draft content specifications from the Smarter Balanced Assessment Consortium (Hess, 2012) indicate that the use of narrative strategies may be part of the scoring criteria for persuasive or informative constructed-response writing items. This means that when writing to argue or to inform, students who embed appropriate narrative elements, such as descriptive details or sequenced events, will likely strengthen the quality of their writing, since flexibly applying rhetoric to address a given purpose or audience is the hallmark of a successful writer.

The standards under the Text Types and Purposes heading are very specific, and each has numerous components that describe the attributes of that type of writing. These components change across grades, describing proficiency at each grade level for each writing type. As grade-specific qualitative descriptions of student writing, they should prove useful in developing writing rubrics. Some of the attributes described in each standard's components are shared across more than one writing type and standard, while others are specific to that standard alone. The attributes that appear across standards include text introduction, ideas and content, organization, word choice, tone, and conclusion.

Writing arguments

The first standard in the Writing strand is about composing sound arguments on substantive topics and issues. To write effectively, students organize a body of evidence and think critically about how to use it in a formal argument. Appendix A cites a variety of research that identifies argumentation as a key skill for college readiness. It also draws a distinction between argument and persuasion. While argument is solely about making appeals to logic, persuasion also includes appeals to emotion and ethics. Lack of reference to persuasion in the standards adds emphasis to the relative importance of evidence-based arguments, but students will need to call upon a range of rhetorical skills to serve a variety of purposes and audiences. Indeed, students must recognize emotional and ethical appeals in the arguments and texts that they analyze and construct, as well as understand the difference between facts and opinions. Figure 3.1 shows Writing Standard 1 (W.1) across the 9–10 and 11–12 grade bands.

Although students have learned in earlier grades to support their opinions with evidence, their writing in high school should be more substantive, and their arguments need to be more formal and complex. Students must learn a great deal about the issue or text that is the subject of their argument, not only to identify opposing viewpoints but also to investigate them for the purpose of developing counterclaims. The breadth of knowledge required of students in this standard suggests that it is best paired with the research standards, which are described later in this chapter.

While freshmen and sophomores analyze the relationships between various positions and the evidence base for each, juniors and seniors go on to establish the significance of claims and develop counterclaims derived from a thorough knowledge base; they sequence content to build a logical argument and consider the values and possible biases of their audience. Furthermore, students in grades 11–12 use syntax purposefully when structuring their writing, a skill that is also emphasized at this level in the Language strand and in other writing standards.

Writing informative or explanatory texts

Writing about information helps students build knowledge across a wide spectrum of topics and subjects. It complements the Common Core reading standards that ask students not only to comprehend key ideas and details but also to integrate, connect, and analyze information from multiple sources and perspectives. By writing explanatory texts, students exhibit their ability to think critically about information.

Figure 3.1 │ **Writing Standard 1: Text Types and Purposes—Argumentation**	
Grades 9–10 Students:	Grades 11–12 Students:
W.1 Write arguments to support claims **in an analysis of substantive topics or texts, using valid reasoning** and relevant and **sufficient** evidence. a. Introduce **precise** claim(s), distinguish the claim(s) from alternate or opposing claims, and **create an organization that establishes clear relationships among claim(s), counterclaims, reasons, and evidence.** b. **Develop** claim(s) **and counterclaims fairly, supplying evidence for each while pointing out the strengths and limitations of both in a manner that anticipates the audience's knowledge level and concerns.** c. Use words, phrases, and clauses **to link the major sections of the text,** create cohesion, and clarify the relationships between claim(s) and reasons, **between reasons and evidence, and between claim(s) and counterclaims.** d. Establish and maintain a formal style **and objective tone while attending to the norms and conventions of the discipline in which they are writing.** e. Provide a concluding statement or section that follows from and supports the argument presented.	**W.1** Write arguments to support claims in an analysis of substantive topics or texts, using valid reasoning and relevant and sufficient evidence. a. Introduce precise, **knowledgeable** claim(s), **establish the significance of the claim(s)**, distinguish the claim(s) from alternate or opposing claims, and create an organization that **logically sequences** claim(s), counterclaims, reasons, and evidence. b. Develop claim(s) and counterclaims fairly **and thoroughly,** supplying **the most relevant** evidence for each while pointing out the strengths and limitations of both in a manner that anticipates the audience's knowledge level, concerns, **values, and possible biases.** c. Use words, phrases, and clauses **as well as varied syntax** to link the major sections of the text, create cohesion, and clarify the relationships between claim(s) and reasons, between reasons and evidence, and between claim(s) and counterclaims. d. Establish and maintain a formal style and objective tone while attending to the norms and conventions of the discipline in which they are writing. e. Provide a concluding statement or section that follows from and supports the argument presented.

Note: Boldface text identifies content that differs from the prior grade level.

The second standard under the Text Types and Purposes heading, Writing Standard 2 (W.2), focuses on writing expository texts (see Figure 3.2).

Figure 3.2	**Writing Standard 2: Text Types and Purposes—Exposition**	
Grades 9–10 Students:	Grades 11–12 Students:

W.2 Write informative/explanatory texts to examine and convey **complex** ideas, concepts, and information **clearly and accurately** through the **effective** selection, organization, and analysis of content.
    a. Introduce a topic; organize **complex** ideas, concepts, and information **to make important connections and distinctions;** include formatting (e.g., headings), graphics (e.g., **figures,** tables), and multimedia when useful to aiding comprehension.
    b. Develop the topic with well-chosen, relevant, and **sufficient** facts, **extended** definitions, concrete details, quotations, or other information and examples **appropriate to the audience's knowledge of the topic.**
    c. Use appropriate and varied transitions to **link the major sections of the text**, create cohesion, and clarify the relationships among **complex** ideas and concepts.
    d. Use precise language and domain-specific vocabulary to **manage the complexity of the topic.**
    e. Establish and maintain a formal style **and objective tone while attending to the norms and conventions of the discipline in which they are writing.**
    f. Provide a concluding statement or section that follows from and supports the information or explanation presented **(e.g., articulating implications or the significance of the topic).**
	W.2 Write informative/explanatory texts to examine and convey complex ideas, concepts, and information clearly and accurately through the effective selection, organization, and analysis of content.
	    a. Introduce a topic; organize complex ideas, concepts, and information **so that each new element builds on that which precedes it to create a unified whole;** include formatting (e.g., headings), graphics (e.g., figures, tables), and multimedia when useful to aiding comprehension.
	    b. Develop the topic **thoroughly by selecting the most significant** and relevant facts, extended definitions, concrete details, quotations, or other information and examples appropriate to the audience's knowledge of the topic.
	    c. Use appropriate and varied transitions **and syntax** to link the major sections of the text, create cohesion, and clarify the relationships among complex ideas and concepts.
	    d. Use precise language, domain-specific vocabulary, **and techniques such as metaphor, simile, and analogy** to manage the complexity of the topic.
	    e. Establish and maintain a formal style and objective tone while attending to the norms and conventions of the discipline in which they are writing.
	    f. Provide a concluding statement or section that follows from and supports the information or explanation presented (e.g., articulating implications or the significance of the topic).

Note: Boldface text identifies content that differs from the prior grade level.	

Appendix A of the standards document describes a variety of genres that should be included in expository writing, such as academic reports, analyses, summaries, workplace documents, and functional writing. Subjects that students address when writing informational texts become increasingly complex in high school, and students should select and structure content carefully in order to clearly convey information in their writing. In grades 9–10, students carefully select supporting details, such as extended definitions, which describe a concept in detail or with examples. In grades 11–12, they may need to sort through many details to select the most significant facts that support their topic.

For a lesson addressing Writing Standard 2 at the grades 11–12 level (W.11–12.2), see **Sample Lesson 2.**

Organizing and structuring complex content appropriately is important to ensure clear writing. In grades 9–10, students organize their writing to make important connections and distinctions between concepts. Appendix A states that such connections may include differentiating types or parts of a subject, or comparing ideas and concepts. In grades 11–12, students focus on structuring writing so that pieces work together as a unified whole. As in prior grades, students use transitions to create cohesion and clarify relationships among ideas and concepts; however, in grades 9–10, students think about the overall structure in order to link major sections of works that are becoming more complex. In grades 11–12, students consider and consciously use syntax as a technique to effectively link ideas, a topic closely related to Standard L.3 in the Language strand, which has students learning how to vary syntax for effect (see p. 52). High school students bring closure to their writing by drawing conclusions about the topic, for example, describing the information's potential impact and why it is important.

As subjects increase in complexity, clarity of expression also becomes a primary focus of student writing. When writing informative or explanatory texts, students take great care in selecting words and phrases, including technical and academic vocabulary, to precisely describe complex topics. Increasing vocabulary knowledge and the accurate use of academic terms is a focus of Standard L.6 in the Language strand. In addition, students in grades 11–12 are expected to use figurative language to describe complex topics. Students must conform to the formal tone and style appropriate to writing in informational or explanatory genres. Appendix A notes that conventions of formality vary for different disciplines and domains; the PARCC frameworks document (PARCC, 2011) suggests that students consult style guides as needed to answer questions of appropriate tone and format.

Writing narratives

The third standard under the Text Types and Purposes heading describes narration, or storytelling. Students write about experiences, either real or imaginary. In contrast to the first two writing types, narration is structured by time and place. Students use a variety of techniques in narrative writing and should become more adept at applying these techniques in their high school years. Narrative writing may serve a variety of purposes and appear in a variety of formats, including narrative poems, essays, and short stories. Such writing increases students' appreciation of the literary techniques they encounter when reading, which suggests that students may benefit from studying the content in standards under the Craft and Structure heading of the Reading Standards for Literature (RL.4–RL.6) as they learn how and where to employ these techniques (see p. 18). Narrative writing also provides students with the opportunity to engage in their learning by expressing their personal ideas, culture, and experiences. Figure 3.3 shows the sequence of Writing Standard 3 (W.3) across the 9–10 and 11–12 grade bands.

Students in high school write narratives that increasingly reflect the literary devices and techniques that they analyze when reading. Students in grades 9–10 are able to guide their readers through multiple plot lines and move between different points of view. Students sequence events and select words and details for the best effect. They can also write conclusions that reflect on the meaning of their narrative. This standard is largely verbatim across grade bands, though students in grades 11–12 are better able to convey the significance of the events and use sequencing that builds toward the desired mood and outcome.

Figure 3.3 | **Writing Standard 3: Text Types and Purposes—Narration**	
Grades 9–10 Students:	Grades 11–12 Students:

W.3 Write narratives to develop real or imagined experiences or events using effective technique, **well-chosen** details, and well-structured event sequences.
    a. Engage and orient the reader by **setting out a problem, situation, or observation, establishing one or multiple point(s) of view, and introducing a narrator and/or characters; create a smooth progression of experiences or events.**
    b. Use narrative techniques, such as dialogue, pacing, description, reflection, and **multiple plot lines,** to develop experiences, events, and/or characters.
    c. Use a variety of **techniques to sequence events so that they build on one another to create a coherent whole.**
    d. Use precise words and phrases, **telling** details, and sensory language to **convey a vivid picture of the** experiences, events, **setting,** and/**or characters.**
    e. Provide a conclusion that follows from and reflects on **what is experienced, observed, or resolved over the course of the narrative.**
	W.3 Write narratives to develop real or imagined experiences or events using effective technique, well-chosen details, and well-structured event sequences.
	    a. Engage and orient the reader by setting out a problem, situation, or observation **and its significance,** establishing one or multiple point(s) of view, and introducing a narrator and/or characters; create a smooth progression of experiences or events.
	    b. Use narrative techniques, such as dialogue, pacing, description, reflection, and multiple plot lines, to develop experiences, events, and/or characters.
	    c. Use a variety of techniques to sequence events so that they build on one another to create a coherent whole **and build toward a particular tone and outcome (e.g., a sense of mystery, suspense, growth, or resolution).**
	    d. Use precise words and phrases, telling details, and sensory language to convey a vivid picture of the experiences, events, setting, and/or characters.
	    e. Provide a conclusion that follows from and reflects on what is experienced, observed, or resolved over the course of the narrative.

Note: Boldface text identifies content that differs from the prior grade level.	

Production and Distribution of Writing

While the first group of standards in the Writing strand details the qualities and characteristics of different writing types, the remaining standards focus on writing processes. The three standards under the Production and Distribution of Writing heading, shown in Figure 3.4, address adapting writing to task, purpose, and audience; using the writing process; and using technology.

The first standard here, Writing Standard 4 (W.4), requires that students adapt their writing for specific tasks, purposes, and audiences. It acknowledges that students need to be flexible writers who can adjust their selected details, text structure, and style in a variety of ways to meet the demands of a given task. W.4 is uniform across grades 6–12; the difficulty

W.4–6

Figure 3.4 | **Writing Standards 4–6: Production and Distribution of Writing**

Grades 9–10 Students:	Grades 11–12 Students:
W.4 Produce clear and coherent writing in which the development, organization, and style are appropriate to task, purpose, and audience.	**W.4** Produce clear and coherent writing in which the development, organization, and style are appropriate to task, purpose, and audience.
W.5 Develop and strengthen writing as needed by planning, revising, editing, rewriting, or trying a new approach, focusing on **addressing what is most significant for a specific purpose and audience.**	**W.5** Develop and strengthen writing as needed by planning, revising, editing, rewriting, or trying a new approach, focusing on addressing what is most significant for a specific purpose and audience.
W.6 Use technology, including the Internet, to produce, publish, **and update individual or shared writing products, taking advantage of technology's capacity to link to other information and to display information flexibly and dynamically.**	**W.6** Use technology, including the Internet, to produce, publish, and update individual or shared writing products **in response to ongoing feedback, including new arguments or information.**

Note: Boldface text identifies content that differs from the prior grade level.

of the skill increases with the demands and complexity of the contexts that students address in their writing.

Writing Standard 5 (W.5) focuses on the writing process. While Writing Standard 10 (see p. 40) makes it clear that students need not apply the full writing process to everything they write, students still need practice planning, revising, and editing their written work. The middle school iterations of Writing Standard 5 specify the use of guidance and support from adults and peers during the writing process. The standard at the high school level make no mention of this kind of guidance, a change conveying the expectation that high school students will be able to draft and develop their own work. Although all writers benefit from having an editor, students must be able to produce polished work independently when support is not available. High school students also revise their work with a specific purpose and audience in mind. As is noted in W.5, editing skills should match the convention and grammar rules specified in the language standards.

Finally, Writing Standard 6 (W.6) asks students to use technology to produce and publish their writing. In prior grades, students have used technology to write individually and collaboratively, but high school students are able to take advantage of more aspects of technology, strategically using it to link and display information in dynamic ways. In grades 11–12, students use technology to respond to "ongoing" feedback, which suggests that projects may expand beyond set pieces to continuing or interactive online texts, such as blogs.

Research to Build and Present Knowledge

In the Common Core standards, research is more than a type of assignment; it is described as a set of skills that may be applied, as needed, to many different types of reading, speaking, and writing tasks. Although the standards under the Research to Build and Present Knowledge heading articulate specific aspects of research processes, the basic skill of synthesizing text information from multiple sources is embedded in many different standards across the ELA strands. In response to this emphasis on research skills, both consortia developing assessments for the Common Core have designed items to test students' research skills, including performance-based tasks that ask students to select appropriate sources and synthesize information.

The three standards listed under Research to Build and Present Knowledge, shown in Figure 3.5, address the scope and purpose of research projects, gathering and synthesizing source information, and the use of analytical reading skills to draw text evidence.

Writing Standard 7 (W.7) focuses on the scope and purpose of research projects. There are no differences in this standard across high school grade bands. The Common Core urges teachers not only to conduct large-scale research projects but also to integrate short research activities into more of their lessons. Within the Common Core, students build research skills in earlier grades with short research tasks. High school students continue this practice by applying research skills to short reading and writing activities, but they also engage in extended research projects. This first research standard indicates that high school students should use research to solve problems and to demonstrate a deep understanding of subjects. To accomplish this, students must be flexible and able to adjust their focus and their search for information in reaction to their initial findings.

For a lesson addressing Writing Standard 8 at the grades 9–10 level (W.9–10.8), see **Sample Lesson 3.**

The second standard, Writing Standard 8 (W.8), addresses gathering and searching for information, as well as synthesizing that information using writing. While middle school students practice similar skills, in grades 9–10, the sources that students use are more authoritative. Ninth and 10th grade students are able to conduct advanced searches in library and information databases. Students become more selective in the sources that they use, and they more skillfully integrate that information into the structure and language of their writing. In grades 11–12, students are able to assess the strengths and limitations of their sources for various tasks, purposes, and audiences. Students learn that specific sources are better suited to some contexts than others. They also learn to avoid overreliance on any one source and understand that their evidence is stronger when gleaned from a variety of materials.

Figure 3.5 | **Writing Standards 7–9: Research to Build and Present Knowledge**

Grades 9–10 Students:	Grades 11–12 Students:
W.7 Conduct short **as well as more sustained** research projects to answer a question (including a self-generated question) **or solve a problem; narrow or broaden the inquiry when appropriate; synthesize multiple sources on the subject, demonstrating understanding of the subject under investigation.**	**W.7** Conduct short as well as more sustained research projects to answer a question (including a self-generated question) or solve a problem; narrow or broaden the inquiry when appropriate; synthesize multiple sources on the subject, demonstrating understanding of the subject under investigation.
W.8 Gather relevant information from multiple **authoritative** print and digital sources, using **advanced searches** effectively; assess the **usefulness** of each source **in answering the research question; integrate information into the text selectively to maintain the flow of ideas,** avoiding plagiarism and following a standard format for citation.	**W.8** Gather relevant information from multiple authoritative print and digital sources, using advanced searches effectively; assess the **strengths and limitations** of each source **in terms of the task, purpose, and audience;** integrate information into the text selectively to maintain the flow of ideas, avoiding plagiarism and **overreliance on any one source** and following a standard format for citation.

W.9 Draw evidence from literary or informational texts to support analysis, reflection, and research.
    a. Apply **grades 9–10** *Reading standards* to literature (**e.g., "Analyze how an author draws on and transforms source material in a specific work [e.g., how Shakespeare treats a theme or topic from Ovid or the Bible or how a later author draws on a play by Shakespeare]"**).
    b. Apply **grades 9–10** *Reading standards* to literary nonfiction (e.g., "Delineate and evaluate the argument and specific claims in a text, assessing whether the reasoning is **valid and the evidence is relevant and sufficient; identify false statements and fallacious reasoning"**).
	W.9 Draw evidence from literary or informational texts to support analysis, reflection, and research.
	    a. Apply **grades 11–12** *Reading standards* to literature (**e.g., "Demonstrate knowledge of eighteenth-, nineteenth- and early-twentieth-century foundational works of American literature, including how two or more texts from the same period treat similar themes or topics"**).
	    b. Apply **grades 11–12** *Reading standards* to literary nonfiction (**e.g., "Delineate and evaluate the reasoning in seminal U.S. texts, including the application of constitutional principles and use of legal reasoning [e.g., in U.S. Supreme Court Case majority opinions and dissents] and the premises, purposes, and arguments in works of public advocacy [e.g., The Federalist, presidential addresses]"**).

Note: Boldface text identifies content that differs from the prior grade level.

The final standard under the Research to Build and Present Knowledge heading, Writing Standard 9 (W.9), addresses the use of analytical reading skills to draw evidence from texts. This standard demonstrates how research activities connect to both reading and writing. Students must apply reading skills as they review research sources. They must analyze and evaluate texts in order to synthesize them in their research writing. The reference to reading in the standard underlines the fact that drawing evidence from texts is not only central to the reading standards but also a key aspect of research. Writing Standard 9 is uniform across the high school grades, though the references to the reading standards change to reflect the particular reading standards for each grade span.

Range of Writing

The writing standards conclude with a single standard focused on the variety of writing tasks in which students should engage. Writing Standard 10 (W.10), which is phrased exactly the same across grade bands, is shown in Figure 3.6.

To meet this standard, students need opportunities to write routinely. Writing assignments should be a regular part of classroom activities and should include both extended writing that is improved after reflection and multiple drafts and focused writing tasks that take place in short time frames.

Figure 3.6 | **Writing Standard 10: Range of Writing**

Grades 9–10 Students:	Grades 11–12 Students:
W.10 Write routinely over extended time frames (time for research, reflection, and revision) and shorter time frames (a single sitting or a day or two) for a range of tasks, purposes, and audiences.	**W.10** Write routinely over extended time frames (time for research, reflection, and revision) and shorter time frames (a single sitting or a day or two) for a range of tasks, purposes, and audiences.

Short writing assignments might, for example, ask students to respond to text-dependent questions or to reflect on a particular aspect of an oral or written text. Both consortia developing assessments for the Common Core plan to include a mix of short and long writing tasks; thus, students need to be able to produce a high-quality first draft under a tight deadline, and review and improve their writing through revision processes. Because student writing should address a variety of tasks, purposes, and audiences, students will need multiple opportunities to practice various writing types and forms. Teachers should design writing activities and assignments with a wide range of authentic purposes and audiences in mind.

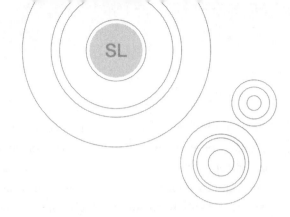

CHAPTER 4

Speaking and Listening

Analyzing spoken messages, communicating with a variety of audiences, and integrating oral, visual, and graphic information are the key skills in the Common Core's Speaking and Listening strand. Although these skills are frequently evaluated in classroom and local assessments, they have not traditionally been included in high-stakes tests. At the time of this writing, both consortia developing assessments for the Common Core plan to include speaking and listening components. As teachers are likely unaccustomed to formal speaking and listening assessments, and because the approaches taken by the consortia differ, the details are worth examining here.

The Partnership for Assessment of Readiness for College and Careers is developing performance-based items to assess oral communication skills, which will be associated with research tasks. PARCC's speaking assessment will be required and will be scored locally by teachers, but it will not be part of students' final summative score (PARCC, 2010). In contrast, the Smarter Balanced Assessment Consortium, according to its draft content specifications for ELA assessments (Hess, 2012), plans to develop short summative speaking assessments that ask students to respond to a prompt. These responses will be recorded and scored externally. Other SBAC assessments will address oral presentation and collaborative discussion skills in connection with investigations or research tasks and will be scored locally by teachers. SBAC's current design calls for scores from these classroom assessments to be "certified" at the district level and reported to the state; recorded student performances will be audited to ensure consistent scoring. SBAC also plans to develop computer-based items to assess student listening skills with nonprint texts.

The standards in the Speaking and Listening strand (SL) are grouped under two headings: Comprehension and Collaboration, and Presentation of Knowledge and Ideas. We'll review each group in turn. It is important to note that, according to the Common Core State Standard Initiative's *Application to Students with Disabilities* (2010b), speaking and listening standards may be applied to the use of sign language for students requiring adaptations.

Comprehension and Collaboration

The Comprehension and Collaboration heading begins with Speaking and Listening Standard 1 (SL.1), which focuses on discussion skills and describes a variety of ways that students learn from each other during thoughtful academic conversations (see Figure 4.1). As compared to their middle school counterparts, high school students exhibit more independence when leading and organizing group work. They conduct research to prepare for discussions, collecting evidence that supports their assertions and broadens all participants' knowledge of the topic. They work with their peers to establish rules and processes that will accomplish their goals.

Although the overall discussion skills described in this first standard are similar across both high school grade bands, each level emphasizes specific aspects. Students in grades 9–10 work together in thoughtful ways, taking time to grasp the ideas of their peers and then collaborating to incorporate those ideas into the group's overall understanding. They agree upon rules for reaching consensus, actively solicit participation from all members, and respond to one another's ideas in ways that propel the conversation and build knowledge around broad themes or large ideas.

SL.1

Figure 4.1	**Speaking and Listening Standard 1: Comprehension and Collaboration—Discussion**	
Grades 9–10 Students:	Grades 11–12 Students:
SL.1 Initiate and participate effectively in a range of collaborative discussions (one-on-one, in groups, and teacher-led) with diverse partners on **grades 9–10** *topics, texts, and issues,* building on others' ideas and expressing their own clearly **and persuasively.** a. Come to discussions prepared, having read **and** researched material under study; explicitly draw on that preparation by referring to evidence from texts **and other research** on the topic or issue **to stimulate a thoughtful, well-reasoned exchange of ideas.** b. **Work with peers to set rules** for collegial discussions and decision-making (**e.g., informal consensus, taking votes on key issues, presentation of alternate views**), clear goals and deadlines, and individual roles as needed. c. **Propel conversations by** posing and responding to questions that relate the current discussion **to broader themes or larger ideas; actively incorporate others into the discussion; and clarify, verify, or challenge ideas and conclusions.** d. **Respond thoughtfully to diverse perspectives, summarize points of agreement and disagreement, and,** when warranted, qualify or justify their own views **and understanding and make new connections in** light of the evidence **and reasoning** presented.	SL.1 Initiate and participate effectively in a range of collaborative discussions (one-on-one, in groups, and teacher-led) with diverse partners on **grades 11–12** *topics, texts, and issues,* building on others' ideas and expressing their own clearly and persuasively. a. Come to discussions prepared, having read and researched material under study; explicitly draw on that preparation by referring to evidence from texts and other research on the topic or issue to stimulate a thoughtful, well-reasoned exchange of ideas. b. Work with peers to **promote civil, democratic** discussions and decision-making, set clear goals and deadlines, and **establish** individual roles as needed. c. Propel conversations by posing and responding to questions that **probe reasoning and evidence; ensure a hearing for a full range of positions on a topic or issue;** clarify, verify, or challenge ideas and conclusions; **and promote divergent and creative perspectives.** d. Respond thoughtfully to diverse perspectives; **synthesize comments, claims, and evidence made on all sides of an issue; resolve contradictions when possible; and determine what additional information or research is required to deepen the investigation or complete the task.**
Note: Boldface text identifies content that differs from the prior grade level.	

Students in grades 11–12 continue these focused conversations and build on the skills practiced in earlier grades. They take further action to ensure that all points of view are considered and all relevant evidence is evaluated. They also seek out different perspectives and identify areas for additional research.

The second and third standards under Comprehension and Collaboration, Speaking and Learning Standard 2 (SL.2) and Standard 3 (SL.3), focus on listening skills. SL.2 addresses integrating and evaluating information from various media, and SL.3 concerns evaluating different aspects of a speaker's presentation (see Figure 4.2).

Standards in prior grades helped students develop the ability to analyze and evaluate information presented in a variety of formats, including

Figure 4.2 | **Speaking and Listening Standards 2–3: Comprehension and Collaboration—Listening**

Grades 9–10 Students:	Grades 11–12 Students:
SL.2 Integrate multiple sources of information presented in diverse media or formats (e.g., visually, quantitatively, orally) evaluating the **credibility and accuracy of each source.**	**SL.2** Integrate multiple sources of information presented in diverse formats and media (e.g., visually, quantitatively, orally) **in order to make informed decisions and solve problems,** evaluating the credibility and accuracy of each source **and noting any discrepancies among the data.**
SL.3 Evaluate a speaker's **point of view,** reasoning, and use of evidence **and rhetoric, identifying any fallacious reasoning or exaggerated or distorted** evidence.	**SL.3** Evaluate a speaker's point of view, reasoning, and use of evidence and rhetoric, **assessing the stance, premises, links among ideas, word choice, points of emphasis, and tone used.**

Note: Boldface text identifies content that differs from the prior grade level.

For a lesson addressing Speaking and Listening Standards 1 and 2 at the grades 11–12 level (SL.11–12.1–2), see **Sample Lesson 2.**

quantitative ones, such as graphs and charts. In high school, SL.2 asks students to build on these skills by integrating information from diverse sources to form in-depth understandings. Thus, multimedia sources enhance the information in print sources, helping students build knowledge on a subject. By grades 11–12, students can use their skills to incorporate a variety of sources in making informed decisions and solving problems. At both levels, as students compare and assimilate information from different media, they consider the credibility and accuracy of each source; in grades 11–12, students note discrepancies among these sources. Although the Common Core includes evaluating *the information* in media sources, the standards do not include evaluating *visual and oral techniques* used in media, such as graphics and sound effects, requirements that are somewhat common in prior state standards documents.

The third standard under this heading, SL.3, focuses on evaluating spoken messages. It applies to a variety of oral texts, including demonstrations and lectures, and is a useful complement to standards in the Reading strand that focus on analyzing historical speeches (RI.9–RI.10, see pp. 23–27). In addition to evaluating the use of logic, reasoning, and evidence in oral texts, which is critical to this standard and many others, high school students also evaluate the use of rhetoric. By grades 11–12, students know how to assess a full range of rhetorical techniques in oral texts.

Presentation of Knowledge and Ideas

As its name implies, the second heading in the Speaking and Listening strand covers standards focused on oral presentation skills. In prior grades, students have learned to present claims and findings using evidence and have refined their speaking skills (e.g., using eye contact and appropriate volume). In high school, students tailor oral presentations to specific circumstances and clearly present information that is becoming increasingly complex. Figure 4.3 shows the sequence of this heading's standards across the grade bands.

Figure 4.3 | **Speaking and Listening Standards 4–6: Presentation of Knowledge and Ideas**

Grades 9–10 Students:	Grades 11–12 Students:
SL.4 Present **information,** findings, and supporting evidence **clearly, concisely, and logically such that listeners can follow the line of** reasoning and the **organization, development, substance, and style are appropriate to purpose, audience, and task.**	**SL.4** Present information, findings, and supporting evidence, **conveying a clear and distinct perspective,** such that listeners can follow the line of reasoning, **alternative or opposing perspectives are addressed,** and the organization, development, substance, and style are appropriate to purpose, audience, and **a range of formal and informal tasks.**
SL.5 Make strategic use of digital media (e.g., textual, graphical, audio, visual, and interactive elements) in presentations **to enhance understanding of findings, reasoning, and evidence** and to add interest.	**SL.5** Make strategic use of digital media (e.g., textual, graphical, audio, visual, and interactive elements) in presentations to enhance understanding of findings, reasoning, and evidence and to add interest.
SL.6 Adapt speech to a variety of contexts and tasks, demonstrating command of formal English when indicated or appropriate.	**SL.6** Adapt speech to a variety of contexts and tasks, demonstrating a command of formal English when indicated or appropriate.

Note: Boldface text identifies content that differs from the prior grade level.

Speaking and Listening Standard 4 (SL.4) is the only standard here that differs between the two high school grade bands. It is focused on the content and organization of student presentations appropriate to purpose, audience, and task. Students in grades 9–10 organize and develop their reasoning and evidence to guide their listeners. In grades 11–12, students become more adept at tailoring the content and organization of their presentations for both formal and informal speaking tasks. They also convey a distinct perspective while addressing alternative perspectives, which is in keeping with SL.1 for grades 11–12.

Speaking and Listening Standard 5 (SL.5) and Standard 6 (SL.6) focus on the format and language used to present information or ideas; these standards do not vary between the high school grade bands. SL.5 addresses the use of digital media. High school students not only must know how to integrate multimedia into presentations but also must be savvy about selecting media that will best convey the information they have to share. The topic of SL.6 is students' ability to adapt their language for different audiences and tasks. Though this standard is uniform across grade bands, the Language strand illustrates how students' ability to use formal English when speaking is expected to improve throughout the high school years. SL.6 highlights the importance of adjusting the formality of oral presentations by using a tone and selecting words that will best engage and influence a given audience. To this end, it emphasizes the need for students to have a variety of opportunities to address different types of audiences and engage in a range of collaborative tasks. Furthermore, the subjects addressed in students' speaking and listening should vary. The SBAC has indicated that the stimuli for their listening and speaking tasks may come from any subject area or content discipline (Hess, 2012). Notably, there are no speaking and listening standards in the set of Common Core standards for literacy in history/ social studies, science, and technical subjects.

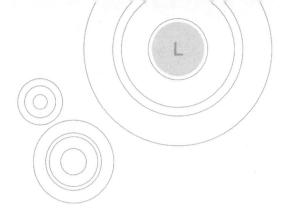

CHAPTER 5

Language

The Language strand (L) focuses on skills related to standard English grammar and usage, vocabulary, sentence fluency, and word choice. Because the skills in this strand support skills described in the Reading, Writing, and Speaking and Listening strands, they are easily addressed in conjunction with other Common Core standards.

The standards within the Language strand are organized under three headings: Conventions of Standard English, Knowledge of Language, and Vocabulary Acquisition and Use.

Conventions of Standard English

There are two standards for Conventions of Standard English. The first, Language Standard 1 (L.1), details grammar and usage conventions for both writing and speaking. The second, Language Standard 2 (L.2), lists grade-level-specific rules and strategies related to capitalization and punctuation. Here at the high school level, L.2 asks students to correctly spell grade-appropriate words. Figure 5.1 shows the sequence of these standards for students in grades 9–10 and 11–12.

L.1–2

Figure 5.1 | Language Standards 1–2: Conventions of Standard English

Grades 9–10 Students:	Grades 11–12 Students:

L.1 Demonstrate command of the conventions of standard English grammar and usage when writing or speaking.
    a. **Use parallel structure.**
    b. **Use various types of phrases (noun, verb, adjectival, adverbial, participial, prepositional, absolute) and clauses (independent, dependent; noun, relative, adverbial) to convey specific meanings and add variety and interest to writing or presentations.**
	L.1 Demonstrate command of the conventions of standard English grammar and usage when writing or speaking.
	    a. **Apply the understanding that usage is a matter of convention, can change over time, and is sometimes contested.**
	    b. **Resolve issues of complex or contested usage, consulting references (e.g., *Merriam-Webster's Dictionary of English Usage, Garner's Modern American Usage*) as needed.**

L.2 Demonstrate command of the conventions of standard English capitalization, punctuation, and spelling when writing.
    a. **Use a semicolon (and perhaps a conjunctive adverb) to link two or more closely related independent clauses.**
    b. **Use a colon to introduce a list or quotation.**
    c. Spell correctly.
	L.2 Demonstrate command of the conventions of standard English capitalization, punctuation, and spelling when writing.
	    a. **Observe hyphenation conventions.**
	    b. Spell correctly.

Note: Boldface text identifies content that differs from the prior grade level.

Because the grammar and convention rules listed in these standards are keyed to each grade level, teachers can see the specific skills that should be their instructional focus. Both the body of the Common Core standards document and Appendix A include a chart showing Language Progressive Skills to provide further support. This chart identifies skills first introduced in lower grades that are likely to require continued attention in higher grades as students are challenged to apply these skills to increasingly sophisticated forms of writing and speaking. A review of the Language Progressive Skills chart can be helpful to high school teachers seeking to differentiate instruction and provide individual students with remediation and foundational skill support as others in the class tackle standards associated with the current grade level.

Note that Language Standard 1 for grades 9–10 focuses on sentence structure, asking students to use parallel structure and various types of phrases and clauses to clearly communicate and engage readers. Such manipulation of sentence structure builds on standards in previous grades; for example, in 7th grade, students choose among sentence types and consider the proper placement of the phrases and clauses that modify other parts of the sentence. Language Standard 2 for grades 9–10 is related to L.1 in that it describes some of the punctuation that is needed when using more complex sentence structures, namely, colons and semicolons.

In grades 11–12, Language Standard 1 requires students to understand that English usage changes over time and is sometimes contested, and to consult references to answer questions they have about complex grammar. By the time students finish high school, they have learned the conventions and rules of grammar and can identify situations in which they might choose to alter traditional usage in order to strengthen the clarity or meaning of their writing. The only punctuation skill specified in Language Standard 2 for grades 11–12 is hyphenation, which implies that by this point in their schooling, students will have already learned all the significant punctuation rules and will have progressed to practicing and perfecting use of punctuation in their writing.

Because grammar and conventions are encountered in all literacy contexts, instruction on and assessment of these skills has commonly been integrated into a wide variety of classroom activities. For example, conventions and grammar are often addressed when students edit their own written assignments (editing is part of the writing process as defined in Writing Standard 5; see pp. 36–37). The SBAC content specifications draft (Hess, 2012) indicates that assessment of conventions may occur within a variety of reading, writing, and speaking tasks, as well as within focused editing tasks and items. The Common Core standards do not dictate a change to the traditional approach of addressing conventions within the writing process; however, because very detailed skills are assigned to specific grades, teachers may need to provide direct instruction on the targeted skills for their grade level. The *PARCC Model Content Frameworks* document (PARCC, 2011) notes that while grammar is meant to be a normal, everyday part of what students do, students should also be taught explicit lessons in grammar as they read, write, and speak.

Knowledge of Language

The Knowledge of Language heading covers only one standard, Language Standard 3 (L.3), shown in Figure 5.2. This standard focuses on students' understanding of how language is selected and structured for different purposes, and on their ability to apply this understanding when constructing or analyzing a text. In prior grades, students learned to apply their

Figure 5.2 | **Language Standard 3: Knowledge of Language**

Grades 9–10 Students:	Grades 11–12 Students:
L.3 Apply knowledge of language **to understand how language functions in different contexts, to make effective choices for meaning or style, and to comprehend more fully** when reading or listening. a. **Write and edit work so that it conforms to the guidelines in a style manual (e.g., *MLA Handbook*, Turabian's *Manual for Writers*) appropriate for the discipline and writing type.**	L.3 Apply knowledge of language to understand how language functions in different contexts, to make effective choices for meaning or style, and to comprehend more fully when reading or listening. a. **Vary syntax for effect, consulting references (e.g., Tufte's *Artful Sentences*) for guidance as needed; apply an understanding of syntax to the study of complex texts when reading.**

Note: Boldface text identifies content that differs from the prior grade level.

knowledge of language to their reading, writing, speaking, and listening, but in high school, students extend this skill to evaluating the effect of authors' language choices for particular contexts and purposes.

This standard has a different focus in each grade band. In grades 9–10, the emphasis is on the use of style manuals when writing. Although many state standards called for the application of a style guide for citations, few required the broader application of those guides for stylistic aspects such as figures and headings, as L.3 for grades 9–10 does. Here, students consider how the various aspects within a given style manual might apply to the type of writing they are doing and make conscious decisions about the format and style of their work. The focus of L.3 for grades 11–12 is syntax. Students study how authors place phrases within sentences to emphasize key points, to create a desired rhythm and tone, or to replicate a particular dialect. When revising their writing, students consider the structure of the language they are using and how they might vary it to create a desired effect. This skill is first introduced in grade 6, when students learn to vary sentence patterns to convey different meanings, appeal to different reader and listener interests, and communicate in different styles. As students' writing matures in high school, they are able to arrange sentences for more complex purposes and for the greatest impact.

Vocabulary Acquisition and Use

As noted in Appendix A of the standards document, research supports vocabulary acquisition as a key element in student academic success. The three standards listed under the Vocabulary Acquisition and Use heading describe strategies for comprehending words and phrases encountered in texts, analysis of figurative meanings and word relationships, and the expansion of students' working vocabulary. Much of these standards' content is identical, not only across the two high school grade bands but also to the middle school standards that precede them. That is not to say that student vocabulary skills are expected to stagnate—far from it. As the complexity of the texts that students encounter increases, so do the demands on students' working vocabulary. High school students may apply the same essential strategies for vocabulary acquisition as in prior grades, but they apply these strategies to words that increasingly rise to the college and career readiness level. It should be noted that the standards under this heading are more detailed than, yet address similar content to, Reading Standard 4, which requires the analysis of words and phrases in a text. Figure 5.3 shows the sequence of standards under the Vocabulary Acquisition and Use heading for grades 9–10 and 11–12.

Figure 5.3 | Language Standards 4–6: Vocabulary Acquisition and Use

Grades 9–10 Students:	Grades 11–12 Students:

L.4 Determine or clarify the meaning of unknown and multiple-meaning words and phrases based on *grades 9–10 reading and content,* choosing flexibly from a range of strategies.
 	
    a. Use context (e.g., the overall meaning of a sentence, paragraph, **or text;** a word's position or function in a sentence) as a clue to the meaning of a word or phrase.
    b. **Identify and correctly use patterns of word changes that indicate different meanings or parts of speech (e.g., *analyze, analysis, analytical; advocate, advocacy*).**
    c. Consult general and specialized reference materials (e.g., dictionaries, glossaries, thesauruses), both print and digital, to find the pronunciation of a word or determine or clarify its precise meaning, its part of speech, **or its etymology.**
    d. Verify the preliminary determination of the meaning of a word or phrase (e.g., by checking the inferred meaning in context or in a dictionary).
	L.4 Determine or clarify the meaning of unknown and multiple-meaning words and phrases based on *grades 11–12 reading and content*, choosing flexibly from a range of strategies.
	
	    a. Use context (e.g., the overall meaning of a sentence, paragraph, or text; a word's position or function in a sentence) as a clue to the meaning of a word or phrase.
	    b. Identify and correctly use patterns of word changes that indicate different meanings or parts of speech (**e.g., *conceive, conception, conceivable***).
	    c. Consult general and specialized reference materials (e.g., dictionaries, glossaries, thesauruses), both print and digital, to find the pronunciation of a word or determine or clarify its precise meaning, its part of speech, its etymology, **or its standard usage.**
	    d. Verify the preliminary determination of the meaning of a word or phrase (e.g., by checking the inferred meaning in context or in a dictionary).

Figure 5.3 ǀ **Language Standards 4–6: Vocabulary Acquisition and Use** *(continued)*	
Grades 9–10 Students:	Grades 11–12 Students:
L.5 Demonstrate understanding of figurative language, word relationships, and nuances in word meanings. 　　a. Interpret figures of speech (e.g., **euphemism, oxymoron**) in context **and analyze their role in the text.** 　　b. **Analyze nuances in the meaning of words with similar denotations.**	**L.5** Demonstrate understanding of figurative language, word relationships, and nuances in word meanings. 　　a. Interpret figures of speech (e.g., **hyperbole, paradox**) in context and analyze their role in the text. 　　b. Analyze nuances in the meaning of words with similar denotations.
L.6 Acquire and use accurately general academic and domain-specific words and phrases, **sufficient for reading, writing, speaking, and listening at the college and career readiness level; demonstrate independence in** gathering vocabulary knowledge when considering a word or phrase important to comprehension or expression.	**L.6** Acquire and use accurately general academic and domain-specific words and phrases, sufficient for reading, writing, speaking, and listening at the college and career readiness level; demonstrate independence in gathering vocabulary knowledge when considering a word or phrase important to comprehension or expression.

Note: Boldface text identifies content that differs from the prior grade level.

The first standard here, Language Standard 4 (L.4), describes strategies for comprehending words and phrases found within oral or written texts. Students choose among vocabulary strategies, such as using context clues, derivations, and reference materials. Though many of these skills have been practiced in earlier grades, the ability to understand new words based on related forms of the word—derivation—is not required before grades 9–10, nor is the use of reference materials to study etymology. In grades 11–12, students extend their use of reference materials to answer questions about a word's correct usage.

For a lesson addressing Language Standard 4 at the grades 11–12 level (L.11–12.4), see **Sample Lesson 2.**

Language Standard 5 (L.5) addresses the analysis of figurative language and the relationships between words with similar meanings. The examples provided for figures of speech are specific to each grade level. While students interpret figures of speech in earlier grades, investigation of how such expressions support the overall text begins in high school. Similarly, while students in 8th grade compare words with similar denotations, high school students examine the effect of word choices in more depth. This standard underlines the importance of students making connections to newly learned words in order to internalize their meaning and understand the multiple ways that these words can be used.

The final standard under Vocabulary Acquisition and Use, Language Standard 6 (L.6), addresses students' working vocabulary. As Appendix A notes, the Common Core emphasizes academic vocabulary (words common across a variety of scholarly writings but rarely found in speech) and domain-specific words (words related to subject-area topics). It's expected that high school students will be more independent in their ability to acquire new vocabulary than younger students. However, teachers should still plan to expose students to academic and domain-specific words in multiple authentic contexts and to give students, particularly English language learners, some direct instruction on target words.

CHAPTER 6

Guidance for Instructional Planning

In this chapter, we provide a brief tutorial on designing lesson plans featuring the types of instructional strategies that appear in this guide's sample lessons. It includes a step-by-step outline for the development of lessons that make best use of proven instructional strategies and will help you ensure students master the new and challenging content represented by the Common Core standards.

The Framework for Instructional Planning

To identify and use effective strategies to develop these lessons, we draw on the instructional planning framework developed for *Classroom Instruction That Works, 2nd edition* (Dean et al., 2012), presented in Figure 6.1.

The Framework organizes nine categories of research-based strategies for increasing student achievement into three components. These components focus on three key aspects of teaching and learning: creating an environment for learning, helping students develop understanding, and helping students extend and apply knowledge. Let's take a close look at each.

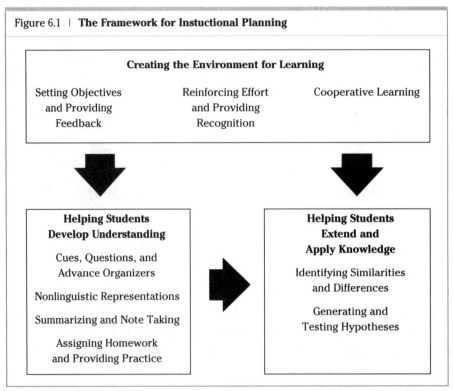

Figure 6.1 | **The Framework for Instuctional Planning**

Creating the Environment for Learning

Setting Objectives and Providing Feedback

Reinforcing Effort and Providing Recognition

Cooperative Learning

Helping Students Develop Understanding

Cues, Questions, and Advance Organizers

Nonlinguistic Representations

Summarizing and Note Taking

Assigning Homework and Providing Practice

Helping Students Extend and Apply Knowledge

Identifying Similarities and Differences

Generating and Testing Hypotheses

Source: From *Classroom Instruction That Works, 2nd ed.* (p. xvi) by Ceri Dean, Elizabeth Hubbell, Howard Pitler, and Bj Stone, 2012, Alexandria, VA: ASCD; and Denver, CO: McREL. Copyright 2012 by McREL. Adapted with permission.

Creating the environment for learning

Teachers create a positive environment for learning when they ensure that students are motivated and focused, know what's expected of them, and regularly receive feedback on their progress. When the environment is right, students are actively engaged in their learning and have multiple opportunities to share and discuss ideas with their peers.

A number of instructional strategies that help create a positive environment for learning may be incorporated into the lesson design itself. Other aspects, such as reinforcing effort and providing recognition, may not be a formal part of the lesson plan but are equally important. The following strategies are essential for creating a positive environment for learning:

- Setting objectives and providing feedback
- Reinforcing effort and providing recognition
- Cooperative learning

Helping students develop understanding

This component of the Framework focuses on strategies that are designed to help students work with what they already know and help them integrate new content with their prior understanding. To ensure that students study effectively outside class, teachers also need strategies that support constructive approaches to assigning homework. The strategies that help students develop understanding include the following:

- Cues, questions, and advance organizers
- Nonlinguistic representations
- Summarizing and note taking
- Assigning homework and providing practice

Helping students extend and apply knowledge

In this component of the Framework, teachers use strategies that prompt students to move beyond the "right answers," engage in more complex reasoning, and consider the real-world connections and applications of targeted content and skills, all of which help students gain flexibility when it comes to using what they have learned. The following strategies help students extend and apply knowledge:

- Identifying similarities and differences
- Generating and testing hypotheses

Figure 6.2 illustrates the three major components of teaching and learning described in *Classroom Instruction That Works*, along with the nine types, or categories, of strategies that further define the components. Taken

Figure 6.2 । Framework Components and the Associated Categories of Instuctional Strategies		
Component	Category	Definition
Creating the Environment for Learning	Setting Objectives and Providing Feedback	Provide students with a direction for learning and with information about how well they are performing relative to a particular learning objective so they can improve their performance.
	Reinforcing Effort and Providing Recognition	Enhance students' understanding of the relationship between effort and achievement by addressing students' attitudes and beliefs about learning. Provide students with non-material tokens of recognition or praise for their accomplishments related to the attainment of a goal.
	Cooperative Learning	Provide students with opportunities to interact with one another in ways that enhance their learning.
Helping Students Develop Understanding	Cues, Questions, and Advance Organizers	Enhance students' ability to retrieve, use, and organize what they already know about a topic.
	Nonlinguistic Representations • Graphic Organizers • Pictures and Pictographs • Mental Images • Kinesthetic Movement • Models/Manipulatives	Enhance students' ability to represent and elaborate on knowledge using mental images.
	Summarizing and Note Taking	Enhance students' ability to synthesize information and organize it in a way that captures the main ideas and supporting details.
	Providing Practice, and Assigning Homework	Extend the learning opportunities for students to practice, review, and apply knowledge. Enhance students' ability to reach the expected level of proficiency for a skill or process

Figure 6.2	**Framework Components and the Associated Categories of Instuctional Strategies** *(continued)*	
Component	Category	Definition
Helping Students Extend and Apply Knowledge	Identifying Similarities and Differences • Comparing • Classifying • Creating/Using Metaphors • Creating/Using Analogies	Enhance students' understanding of and ability to use knowledge by engaging them in mental processes that involve identifying ways in which items are alike and different.
	Generating and Testing Hypotheses	Enhance students' understanding of and ability to use knowledge by engaging them in mental processes that involve making and testing hypotheses.

Source: From *Classroom Instruction That Works, 2nd ed.* (p. xviii) by Ceri Dean, Elizabeth Hubbell, Howard Pitler, and Bj Stone, 2012, Alexandria, VA: ASCD; and Denver, CO: McREL. Copyright 2012 by McREL. Adapted with permission.

together, this information can point you toward activities that will suit your learning objectives and support your students' success.

Lesson Development, Step by Step

To help you get started developing lessons that incorporate these strategies, we provide a step-by-step process to ensure that you've had an opportunity to consider where within a lesson the various strategies might be used most effectively. Those steps are as follows:

1. Identify the focus for the lesson.
2. Determine how learning will be assessed.
3. Determine the activities that will start the lesson.
4. Determine the activities that will engage students in learning the content.
5. Determine the activities that will close the lesson.

Let's look now at the details of each step and how you might incorporate the nine effective instructional strategies associated with each of the

Framework's three components. We'll reference the sample lessons in this guide to illustrate particular aspects of this approach.

Step 1: Identify the focus for the lesson

The critical first step in crafting a lesson is to identify what students should learn as a result of their engagement in the lesson activities. Setting objectives for students also means establishing the guidelines for your development of the lesson: namely, that you will select and develop only those activities that will help students meet the objectives set. A learning objective is built directly from a standard; the objectives found in this guide's sample lessons are constructed from Common Core standards and listed under the heading "Common Core State Standards—Knowledge and Skills to Be Addressed."

Clarifying learning objectives. To ensure that students are clear about what they will learn, you will want your lesson plans to include more specific statements of the objectives in clear, student-friendly language. Some teachers accomplish this by using stems such as "I can . . ." or "We will be able to . . ." or "Students will be able to . . ." and providing a paraphrased version of the standard, simplifying the language as necessary. In the sample lessons for this guide, such specifics may be found under the headings "Knowledge/Vocabulary Objectives" and "Skill/Process Objectives" and prefaced by either "Students will understand . . ." or "Students will be able to. . . ."

Identifying essential questions and learning objectives. Framing the lesson's objectives under a broader essential question provides students with alternate avenues to find personal relevance and can energize them to seek answers as they begin a unit or lesson. The essential question properly focuses on the broader purpose of learning, and it is most effective when it is open-ended and not a question that can be easily answered. Each of the sample lessons includes an essential question—the learning objectives reframed to clarify for students what value the lesson holds for them.

Identifying foundational knowledge and possible misconceptions related to the learning objectives. As you develop learning objectives for a lesson, consider the other skills students will need to use but that will not be the explicit focus of instruction or assessment. Our discussions of each standard in this guide identify the critical knowledge and skills that students are assumed to have mastered or practiced in lessons prior to learning the new content. In the sample lessons, you'll find these standards under the heading "Common Core State Standards—Prior Knowledge and Skills to Be Applied."

Step 2: Determine how learning will be assessed

As important as identifying the learning objective for a lesson is identifying the criteria you will use to determine if students have met that objective. You will want to be clear about the rigor identified in the Common Core standards. As you develop scoring tools, such as checklists and rubrics that define the various levels of performance related to the objective's knowledge or skill, it is important to review the details of the objective's underlying standard to be sure you are looking for the appropriate level of mastery.

Assessing prior knowledge. Step 2 involves planning how to measure students' prior knowledge, especially the knowledge identified in Step 1 as prerequisite to mastery of the learning objective. For example, you might ask students to complete a short problem or share reflections on their prior experiences with similar tasks. This approach may also surface any lingering student misconceptions that you'll want to address before proceeding.

Providing feedback. This part of the planning process also includes deciding how you will provide students with feedback on their progress toward the outcome. Providing feedback is an important aspect of creating the environment for learning because understanding what good performance looks like, how to judge their own performance relative to a benchmark, and what they need to do to improve their performance helps students develop a sense of control over their learning. During lesson planning, you might also consider how peers can give their classmates feedback on progress toward the stated objective.

Step 3: Determine the activities that will start the lesson

Step 3 of the planning process concerns the sequence of activities at the start of the lesson, which relate to the "Creating the Environment for Learning" component of the Framework for Instructional Planning. The beginning of each lesson should be orchestrated to capture students' interest, communicate the learning objectives, and encourage their commitment to effort.

Communicating learning objectives. You can share learning objectives by stating them orally, but be sure to post them in writing for reference throughout the lesson. Doing so not only reminds the class of the objectives' importance but also ensures that even students who weren't paying close attention or who came in late can identify what they are working to achieve.

Identifying the essential question and providing a context. Students engage in learning more readily when they can see how it connects to their own interests. The essential question you provide at the beginning of the lesson helps orient them to the purpose for learning. Students will also have a greater sense of involvement if you share with them what activities they'll be engaged in and how these activities will help build their understanding and skill. The sample lessons in this guide present this preview under the heading "Activity Description to Share with Students." It is something you might read aloud or post, along with the objectives and essential questions, as you create the environment for learning at the beginning of a lesson. To encourage greater involvement, you might also ask students to set personal goals based on the learning objectives in each activity. These personal goals may translate the learning objective to immediate goals that resonate for each student.

Reinforcing effort. As you develop the activities for the lesson, look for natural points where you might build in opportunities for students to receive encouragement they need to continue their work. To reinforce student effort, we need to help students understand the direct connection between how hard they work and what they achieve. It's another way in which teachers can provide students with a greater sense of control over their own learning.

Step 4: Determine the activities that will engage students in learning the content

At Step 4 we are at the crux of the lesson, deciding what students will do to acquire, extend, and apply knowledge or skills. This stage of planning includes identifying when formative assessment should take place, when you will provide students feedback from the assessment, and how you will ensure that students have a clear understanding of how they are doing. And, of course, you will need to decide which instructional activities will best serve the lesson's primary purposes, considering whether the activities need to focus on helping students acquire new knowledge and skill or help them extend and refine what they've already learned.

Choosing activities and strategies that develop student understanding. When your aim is to help students understand new information or a new process, then you will want to design activities that incorporate strategies associated with that component of the Framework for Instructional Planning. These are the strategies that help students access prior knowledge and organize new learning. Students come to every lesson with some prior knowledge, and the effective use of strategies such as using cues, questions, and advance organizers can enhance students' ability to retrieve and use what they already know about a topic in order to access something new. You can help students access and leverage their prior knowledge through simple discussion, by providing "KWL"-type advance organizers, by having students read or listen to short texts related to the targeted content, or any of a number of ways. Activities incorporating the use of nonlinguistic representations (including visualization) in which students elaborate on knowledge, skills, and processes are other good ways to help students integrate new learning into existing knowledge. The strategies of note taking and summarizing also support students' efforts to synthesize information through the act of organizing it in a way that captures its main ideas and supporting details or highlights key aspects of new processes. Finally, homework can help students learn or review new content and practice skills so that they can more quickly reach the expected level of proficiency. However, you will want to think carefully about your homework practices, as the research on what makes homework effective shows mixed results. Dean and colleagues (2012) recommend that teachers design homework assignments that directly support learning objectives. Students need to understand how homework serves lesson objectives, and once homework is completed, it is important that teachers provide feedback on the assignment.

Choosing activities and strategies that help students extend and apply knowledge. When your aim is to help students extend or apply their knowledge or master skills and processes, they will need opportunities to practice independently. What are beneficial are activities that ask them to make comparisons, classify, and create using metaphors and analogies. Research summarized in the second edition of *Classroom Instruction That Works* indicates that these strategies, associated with the "Helping Students Extend and Apply Knowledge" component of the Framework for Instructional Planning, are a very worthwhile use of instructional time. They help raise students' levels of understanding and improve students' ability to use what they learn. Because students need to understand the concepts or skills that they're applying, it's better to incorporate these kinds of practice and application activities later in a lesson than at the lesson's outset.

Remember, too, that strategies that help students generate and test hypotheses are not meant just for science classrooms. They are a way to deepen students' knowledge by requiring them to use critical-thinking skills, such as analysis and evaluation.

Grouping students for activities. Cooperative learning can be tremendously beneficial, whether students are developing a new skill or understanding or applying or extending it. With every lesson you design, consider when it makes sense to use this strategy, what kind of student grouping will be most beneficial, and how these groups should be composed. Cooperative learning is a strong option, for example, when you want to differentiate an activity based on student readiness, interest, or learning style. Consider, too, that students' learning experiences will be different depending on whether you permit them to self-select into groups of their choosing or assign their group partners, whether the groups are larger (four or five students) or smaller (e.g., pair work), and whether these groups are homogeneous or heterogeneous.

Providing students with the opportunity to share and discuss their ideas with one another in varying cooperative learning arrangements lays a foundation for the world beyond school, which depends on people working interdependently to solve problems and to innovate. Interacting with one another also deepens students' knowledge of the concepts they are learning; in other words, talking about ideas and listening to others' ideas helps students understand a topic and retain what they've learned, and it may send their thinking in interesting new directions.

Step 5: Determine the activities that will close the lesson

Bringing the lesson to a close provides an opportunity for you and students to look back on and sum up the learning experience.

During this part of the lesson, you want to return to the learning objectives and confirm that you have addressed each of them. This can be approached in one or more ways—through informal sharing, formative assessment, or even summative assessment. Students benefit from the opportunity to gauge their progress in learning. You might prompt them to reflect on the lesson in a journal entry, learning log, or response card, which can easily serve as an informal check for understanding. Note that asking students to share what they found most difficult as well as what worked well can provide you with insight you can apply during the next lesson and can use to refine the lesson just completed.

Depending upon the nature of the objective and whether the lesson appears late in the unit, you may elect to conduct a formal summative assessment. Alternatively, you may identify a homework assignment tied to the learning objective, making sure that students understand how the assignment will help them deepen their understanding or develop their skill.

✳✳✳

In the remaining pages of this guide, we offer sample lesson plans based on the Common Core State Standards for English Language Arts, the Framework for Instructional Planning, and the steps just outlined.

Is This Source Credible? Useful? Why and Why Not?

Grade Level/Course: ELA grades 9–10
Length of Lesson: Two hours; two 60-minute class periods

Introduction

To prepare for college and careers, students need to have experience in researching subjects from all areas of the curriculum. The standards for student research are described in the Common Core's Writing strand. These standards emphasize using both short and more sustained research projects to answer a question, assess the usefulness of sources, gather information from multiple sources, and synthesize that information, thereby demonstrating understanding of the subject under investigation.

Because the Internet has become a valuable research tool, it is important for students to know how to evaluate any websites they find on a given subject. In this lesson, students will need access to computers and the Internet. Students will learn how to evaluate the usefulness of a variety of Internet sources on the Nazi regime in the 1930s and 1940s as a prelude to future lessons, in which they will conduct research that builds on their background knowledge of Nazi Germany. Students will then use their research to analyze how an author uses historical fact to tell a story.

Strategies from the Framework for Instructional Planning

- *Creating the Environment for Learning:* The lesson's learning objective ("To determine if a website used for research on a selected topic is credible and useful") is central to the lesson content. The teacher models using questions to evaluate a website, and then students, working cooperatively, use the same questions to evaluate a different website. The teacher gives individual praise and recognition to students for bringing in websites to evaluate. Cooperative learning takes place several times via small-group work and partner sharing.

- *Helping Students Develop Understanding:* Several strategies support the development of students' understanding. The teacher models how to use the questions to evaluate a website and then encourages students to work together to develop their questioning skills. Students then write a claim about which websites are credible, using examples from the websites to explore the meaning of the word "credible." Students use a graphic organizer as they independently work on evaluating websites connected to the Nazi era, and then the teacher allows time for students to share their learning and opinions about the websites.

- *Helping Students Extend and Apply Knowledge:* Activities that ask students to evaluate the credibility of the websites they find on Nazi Germany provide opportunity for students to extend and apply their new knowledge about what makes a website credible to their own research. They will have the opportunity to extend this knowledge further in subsequent lessons as they pull actual research from the credible websites to analyze how authors use facts to tell a story.

Common Core State Standards—Knowledge and Skills to Be Addressed

Strand/Domain: Reading—Informational Text

Heading: Integration of Knowledge and Ideas
RI.9–10.8 Delineate and evaluate the argument and specific claims in a text, assessing whether the reasoning is valid and the evidence is relevant and sufficient; identify false statements and fallacious reasoning.

Strand: Writing

Heading: Research to Build and Present Knowledge

W.9–10.8 Gather relevant information from multiple authoritative print and digital sources, using advanced searches effectively; assess the usefulness of each source in answering the research question; integrate information into the text selectively to maintain the flow of ideas, avoiding plagiarism and following a standard format for citation.

Strand: Speaking and Listening

Heading: Comprehension and Collaboration

SL.9–10.2 Integrate multiple sources of information presented in diverse media or formats (e.g., visually, quantitatively, orally), evaluating the credibility and accuracy of each source.

Common Core State Standards—Prior Knowledge and Skills to Be Applied

Strand/Domain: Reading—Informational Text

Heading: Craft and Structure

RI.9–10.6 Determine an author's point of view or purpose in a text and analyze how an author uses rhetoric to advance that point of view or purpose.

Teacher's Lesson Summary

In this lesson, students take a list of 15 topics, terms, people, and events mentioned in or inferred from the novel *The Book Thief* by Markus Zusak and conduct an Internet search for websites about those topics. Students determine the usefulness and credibility of the websites they find using a prepared set of website evaluation questions.

Note: After this two-day lesson, students will extend their knowledge by using the websites that they have deemed credible to build their background knowledge about the Nazi regime in the 1930s and 1940s. This research is an early activity in a unit that includes reading *The Book Thief*. Ultimately, students will analyze and make a claim about whether or not Markus Zusak, the author of the book, portrayed history accurately in his story.

Essential Question: How can we identify whether a website is a useful and credible resource?

Learning Objective: To determine if a website used for research on a selected topic is credible and useful.

Knowledge/Vocabulary Objectives

At the conclusion of this lesson, students will

- Understand what is meant by the word "credible" and how it applies to websites.
- Understand the word "valid" as it applies to research.

Skill/Process Objectives

At the conclusion of this lesson, students will be able to

- Evaluate an online resource to determine if it is credible and useful.

Resources/Preparation Needed

1. A list of evaluation questions that students will use to gauge the credibility of websites (see p. 73), one per student

2. A print or electronic graphic organizer keyed to the website evaluation questions and designed to guide students' search for credible and reliable sources of information on 15 topics mentioned in or related to *The Book Thief* (see Figure A, pp. 76–78), one per student

Activity Description to Share with Students

Internet research can be fun, but unless you know how to determine which websites are credible and useful, your research may not be valid. During this lesson, you will determine which websites about the Nazi regime in the 1930s and 1940s are credible and will be useful for your research project about Markus Zusak's novel *The Book Thief*. You will answer a set of questions to determine whether or not the websites you find are credible sources of information that will help you in your project.

Lesson Activity Sequence—Class #1

Start the Lesson

1. Post and discuss the essential question and learning objective.

2. Ask students what they know about the two terms "credible" and "valid." Then have them talk with a partner about websites they have used for research in the past. Did the students think those websites were credible? Was the research they conducted via these websites valid? How do they know?

Engage Students in Learning the Content

1. Introduce and distribute the following website evaluation questions:

   - Who is the author of this website material?
   - What are the author's credentials?
   - Does the author express a certain point of view?
   - Who is the author's intended audience?
   - Can you find a date for this website material?
   - Is the website credible/useful or not credible/useful?

2. Model how to use the questions to analyze one website about Martin Luther King. (You might focus on www.thekingcenter.org or www.martinlutherking. org. These websites are quite different from one another and will serve as good examples for applying the questions.)

3. Next, have students work in small groups, answering the questions as they look at the other website on King.

4. Bring students back together for a full-class discussion about their answers. Discuss the words "credible" and "valid" as they pertain to websites and research.

5. Ask students to do a quick-write using the following prompt: *Make a claim about which website is more credible for researching King's life. Support your argument with several examples.*

Close the Lesson

1. Have students share their quick-writes with a partner, and give and receive feedback. Call for student volunteers to share their quick-writes with the rest of the class, and lead a group discussion of the claims students make.
2. Collect the quick-writes and review them before the next class session to check students' understanding of how to evaluate website credibility and validity.
3. *Homework:* Ask students to find five or six websites with information about Nazi Germany. They should come to class with these URLs and be prepared to evaluate whether the websites are credible and valid or not.

Lesson Activity Sequence—Class #2

Start the Lesson

1. Review the learning objective.
2. Read a few of the quick-writes from the previous day out loud to review how to evaluate a website.
3. Check for homework completion.

Engage Students in Learning the Content

1. Distribute blank copies of the prepared **Graphic Organizer for Website Evaluation** (see **Figure A**, pp. 76–78). Explain to students that you have categorized the questions used during the previous class session and that they will now use these criteria to evaluate the credibility and usefulness of online sources of information about 15 topics addressed in *The Book Thief*.
2. Ask students to use the graphic organizer as they work independently to evaluate some of the URLs gathered for their homework assignment and then proceed to finding additional websites in order to cover all the topics included in the organizer. Note that some websites may be pertinent to several topics on the list. Explain to students that their goal is to find 7–10 credible websites.
3. As students continue to work independently, check in with each to give feedback and recognize effort.

Close the Lesson

1. After 35 minutes, pair students with partners to share findings and give each other feedback on the websites they have assessed.
2. Conduct a quick, whole-class discussion about the credibility of the websites the students have found.
3. *Homework:* Ask students to find at least two more credible websites and two that are not credible for each of the 15 topics. They should bring the additional URLs and evaluations to the next class session.

Additional Resources for This Lesson

Suggested resources for teachers interested in developing their own set of questions for evaluating online sources:

- Purdue University Library, "Evaluating Sources"
  http://gemini.lib.purdue.edu/core/files/evaluating4.html
- Teacher Tap, "Evaluating Internet Resources"
  http://eduscapes.com/tap/topic32.htm
- Education World, "True or False: A Web Literacy Lesson"
  www.educationworld.com/a_lesson/01-1/lp230_05.shtml
- Education World, "A Techtorial"
  www.educationworld.com/a_tech/techtorial/techtorial002j.shtml
- New Mexico State University Library, "Evaluation Criteria"
  http://lib.nmsu.edu/instruction/evalcrit.html
- Phil Bradley's Website, "Fake Websites or Spoof Websites"
  www.philb.com/fakesites.htm

Figure A | Graphic Organizer for Website Evaluation

Key Topics or Terms	Website	Reliability/ Credibility	Perspective/ Bias	Purpose	Date	Credible?
The Nazi Regime (1930s to 1940)	*Website URL*	*Who is the author? What are the author's credentials?*	*Does the author express a certain point of view? What is it?*	*Who is the author's intended audience?*	*Can you find a date for this website material? What is it?*	*Yes/No Why?*
1. Restrictions on and treatment of Jews						
2. Bystanders						
3. Hitler Youth						
4. Stalingrad						

5. Luftwaffe	6. Sondereinheit (LSE)	7. Adolf Hitler	8. Jesse Owens	9. October 7, 1943, bombing of Molching	10. The Star of David

(continued)

Figure A | **Graphic Organizer for Website Evaluation** *(continued)*

Key Topics or Terms	Website	Reliability/ Credibility	Perspective/ Bias	Purpose	Date	Credible?
11. German/ Russian campaign						
12. Dachau						
13. Death marches in Europe						
14. Treatment of people who assist Jews						
15. Nazi soldiers						

Close Reading of and Writing About Poetry

Grade Level/Course: ELA grades 11–12
Length of Lesson: Two hours; two 60-minute class periods (with an optional third 60-minute class period devoted to students' writing)

Introduction

The Common Core emphasizes close reading, which involves readers dissecting and analyzing the specific words, sentences, and structures in a text that they can use to construct meaning. Close reading often requires rereading. Poetry lends itself particularly well to close reading, as repeat encounters often bring fresh insights and a deeper understanding of the poet's craft. The poem at the center of this lesson, which may form part of a unit on poetry from the Romantic Movement, is John Keats's "Ode on a Grecian Urn." It exhibits many of the qualitative dimensions of text complexity described in Appendix A of the Common Core State Standards document, including multiple levels of meaning, extensive figurative language, sophisticated themes, and cultural allusions. "Ode on a Grecian Urn" is also cited in the standards document's Appendix B as a complex text for grades 11–12.

The Common Core standards also emphasize the need for students to write from sources, demonstrating their understanding of text. The literary analysis essay in this lesson asks students to synthesize their ideas about the poem's imagery. Students draw from the graphic organizer used during close reading and from discussions with peers to develop and support their ideas.

Strategies from the Framework for Instructional Planning

- *Creating the Environment for Learning:* The learning objectives ("To determine the meaning and impact of specific words and phrases in a highly regarded poem" and "To write an essay that analyzes the impact of a skilled poet's word choices on imagery in the poem") are central to the content of the lesson. Students give feedback and recognition to one another as they share their graphic organizers. Cooperative learning takes place as students use guiding questions to discuss the poem. The teacher offers feedback by conferring with students as they read the poem closely and work to fill in a graphic organizer and also provides the additional support some students may need to engage with this complex text.

- *Helping Students Develop Understanding:* This lesson features several strategies that help students develop understanding. The teacher uses a nonlinguistic representation (an oral recording of the ode) and a graphic organizer for analyzing specific words and phrases. Small-group and whole-class discussions support students' analysis of a complex text.

- *Helping Students Extend and Apply Knowledge:* Students use what they learned from their close reading of the poem to write an analysis of the poem's imagery.

Common Core State Standards—Knowledge and Skills to Be Addressed

Strand/Domain: Reading—Literature

Heading: Key Ideas and Details
RL.11–12.1 Cite strong and thorough textual evidence to support analysis of what the text says explicitly as well as inferences drawn from the text, including determining where the text leaves matters uncertain.

Heading: Craft and Structure
RL.11–12.4 Determine the meaning of words and phrases as they are used in the text, including figurative and connotative meanings; analyze the impact of specific word choices on meaning and tone, including words with multiple meanings or language that is particularly fresh, engaging, or beautiful. (Include Shakespeare as well as other authors.)

Strand: Writing

Heading: Text Types and Purposes

W.11–12.2 Write informative/explanatory texts to examine and convey complex ideas, concepts, and information clearly and accurately through the effective selection, organization, and analysis of content.

Strand: Speaking and Listening

Heading: Comprehension and Collaboration

SL.11–12.2 Evaluate a speaker's point of view, reasoning, and use of evidence and rhetoric, assessing the stance, premises, links among ideas, word choice, points of emphasis, and tone used.

Strand: Language

Heading: Vocabulary Acquisition and Use

L.11–12.4 Determine or clarify the meaning of unknown and multiple-meaning words and phrases based on grades 11–12 reading and content, choosing flexibly from a range of strategies.

Common Core State Standards—Prior Knowledge and Skills to Be Applied

Strand: Speaking and Listening

Heading: Comprehension and Collaboration

SL.11–12.1 Initiate and participate effectively in a range of collaborative discussions (one-on-one, in groups, and teacher-led) with diverse partners on grades 11–12 topics, texts, and issues, building on others' ideas and expressing their own clearly and persuasively.

SL.11–12.2 Evaluate a speaker's point of view, reasoning, and use of evidence and rhetoric, assessing the stance, premises, links among ideas, word choice, points of emphasis, and tone used.

Strand: Language

Heading: Vocabulary Acquisition and Use

L.11–12.5 Demonstrate understanding of figurative language, word relationships, and nuances in word meanings.

Teacher's Lesson Summary

Students listen to John Keats's "Ode on a Grecian Urn." They read and analyze the poem for words that they don't understand and for words and phrases with strong imagery. Next, students discuss the words and phrases they chose with peers, following a set of guiding questions. Finally, students write a rubric-guided essay on the impact of word choices in the poem, using text evidence to support their analysis.

Essential Question: What effects do a poet's word choices have on meaning and tone in a poem that some consider a masterpiece?

Learning Objectives: (1) To determine the meaning and impact of specific words and phrases in a highly regarded poem. (2) To write an essay that analyzes the impact of a skilled poet's word choices on imagery in the poem.

Knowledge/Vocabulary Objectives

At the conclusion of this lesson, students will

- Understand and explain the meaning of "ekphrasis."
- Understand and explain what an ode is.
- Understand the literary technique of "imagery."
- Understand what a Grecian urn is and what it looks like.
- Understand who and what "the Sylvan historian" is.
- Understand reference to Arcady and Tempe.

Skill/Process Objectives

At the conclusion of this lesson, students will be able to

- Determine how words and phrases can be used effectively in a poem.
- Determine and write about the effective use of imagery in a poem using evidence from the poem.

Resources/Preparation Needed

- Copies of "Ode on a Grecian Urn" by John Keats, one per student. Text is provided on page 158 of Appendix B of the Common Core ELA Standards and is readily available online.

- An audio reading of "Ode on a Grecian Urn," such as the one performed by Tony Britton, available at www.youtube.com/watch?v=3G9jYTR9fEs
- A prepared graphic organizer that students will use to guide their close reading (see Figure A, p. 87), one per student
- A writing rubric focused on the literary analysis of poetry and based on Writing Standard 1 and Language Standard 2 (see Figure B, p. 88), one per student

Activity Description to Share with Students

"Ode on a Grecian Urn" is a famous and complex poem from the Romantic era. We will listen to it together, and you will read it independently multiple times. Using a graphic organizer, you will identify and investigate words that you don't know and words that have imagery. In a group, you will discuss your chosen words and understanding of the poem before writing an essay about the impact of word choices on imagery in the poem.

Lesson Activity Sequence—Class #1

Start the Lesson

1. Post and explain the activity description and learning objectives.
2. Have students turn and talk to each other about their understanding of the objectives. Ask a few volunteers to share their thoughts with the whole class and provide feedback on their current understanding.
3. Introduce Keats's "Ode on a Grecian Urn" by playing the reading of it performed by Tony Britton (or a similar recording). Students should listen and read along with their own copy of the poem.

Engage Students in Learning the Content

1. Explain that analysis of complex texts takes "close reading." Close reading requires a person to read the text multiple times and focus on particular words and phrases.
2. Ask students to define the word "imagery" and discuss why poets try to evoke imagery in poems such as "Ode on a Grecian Urn."

3. Distribute blank copies of the **Graphic Organizer for the Close Reading of Poetry** (see **Figure A**, p. 87), and model for students how they should use it as they read. (The figure includes example responses.)

4. Have students read the poem independently. They should determine the meaning of unfamiliar words using a variety of strategies, including examining the context of the line and stanza and using reference sources. They should then record the meaning on the graphic organizer.

5. As students analyze the poem, they should also use the graphic organizer to identify words and phrases that contain striking imagery, recording the focus of the image, questions they may have about the word or phrase, connections they make with the image, and/or the feelings that the image evokes.

6. As students work, confer with them individually to check their understanding. The Common Core standards note that some students may need scaffolding and support to read complex texts. Be prepared to work more closely with these students as they use their graphic organizers to capture definitions of the lesson's key words and phrases.

Close the Lesson

1. Reconvene as a whole class and have student volunteers share a word or phrase that they identified as containing imagery. Ask whether other students chose the same words and whether they made the same connections and had similar reactions to the word.

2. Ask students to volunteer questions that they have about the poem. Discuss these questions as a whole class.

3. *Homework:* Students should complete the graphic organizer for all the stanzas of the poem if they have not done so.

Lesson Activity Sequence—Class #2
Start the Lesson

1. Review the learning objectives.

2. Once again, play the recording of "Ode on a Grecian Urn," and ask students to review their graphic organizers as they listen.

3. Discuss any new insights students have after hearing the poem again.

Engage Students in Learning the Content

1. Direct students to form small groups and to elect one member who will later summarize their discussion for the whole class.
2. Explain that every group member will share one or more of the words and phrases they included in their graphic organizers and then compare their thoughts and reactions with those of peers who chose the same words and phrases.
3. Ask the student groups to discuss the following guiding questions and record their thoughts:
   a. What attitudes or emotions are expressed by the poem's speaker, and how are those feelings reflected in the images on the urn?
   b. Which images on the urn depict an idealistic world, and which images depict a more realistic view of the world?
4. Conduct the report-out in which one member from each group summarizes the group's discussion for the whole class.
5. Describe the writing assignment to students. Explain that they should write a literary analysis about imagery in "Ode on a Grecian Urn" that cites specific words and phrases as supporting evidence. To develop their ideas, they should review their graphic organizers and ideas gathered through discussions.
6. Provide students with a copy of the **Writing Rubric for Literary Analysis of Poetry** (see **Figure B**, pp. 88–89), and review the standards-based criteria on which they will be scored. You may also share a model of student writing with a similar purpose, using the rubric to discuss the characteristics of a successful literary analysis essay.

Close the Lesson

1. Have students share what they plan to write about with a partner. Ask the pairs to discuss their main idea or thesis for the essay and how quotations from the poem might support it.
2. Remind students about the due date for the essay, including whether they need to write it as homework or whether class time will be given the following day.

Additional Resources for This Lesson

Suggested websites for teachers and students:

- Poets.org, "Notes on Ekphrasis"
  www.poets.org/viewmedia.php/prmMID/19939
- Poets.org, "Poetic Form: Ode"
  www.poets.org/viewmedia.php/prmMID/5784
- Poetry Magic
  www.poetrymagic.co.uk

Figure A	**Graphic Organizer for the Close Reading of Poetry**	
Unknown Words in Poem	**Meaning/Definition**
Ekphrasis	a graphic description of a visual work of art
Ode	a type of poem that speaks to a person or object
Urn	vase
Sylvan historian	someone who knows the history of the forest
Arcady	Arcadia is a peaceful, simple place; a place in Greece
Tempe	a wooded valley in Greece
Words or Phrases with Strong Imagery	**Your Interpretation** (To what does the word or phrase refer? What emotions, connections, or questions does the word or phrase evoke?)
unravish'd bride of quietness	Describes the urn. But why quiet? Shouldn't a bride be full of excitement and joy?
leaf-fring'd legend	Describes decorations on the urn. Legends last through time, but leaves don't . . . except for the leaves on this urn.

Figure B	Writing Rubric for Literary Analysis of Poetry		
Advanced	**Proficient**	**Partially Proficient**	**Novice**
Clearly and effectively introduce the poem and how it uses imagery.	Clearly introduce the poem and how it uses imagery.	Introduce the poem and how it uses imagery in a somewhat unclear manner.	Introduce the poem and how it uses imagery in a vague or confusing manner.
Organize all ideas and minor details so that each idea builds on that which precedes it to create a unified whole that engages and guides the reader.	Organize all major ideas so that each idea builds on that which precedes it to create a unified whole.	Organize ideas so that most ideas build on what precedes them.	Organize ideas in a confusing way or in a way that is hard to follow.
Develop the topic, showing insight in selecting the most significant and effective quotations from the poem as support.	Develop the topic thoroughly by selecting the most significant quotations from the poem as support.	Develop the topic by selecting somewhat relevant quotations from the poem as support.	Ineffectively develop the topic by selecting quotations from the poem that do not clearly provide support.
Use highly effective and varied transitions and syntax to link sections of the text, create cohesion, and clarify the relationships among complex ideas and concepts.	Use appropriate and varied transitions and syntax to link the major sections of the text, create cohesion, and clarify the relationships among complex ideas and concepts.	Use simplistic and a limited variety of transitions and syntax to link the major sections of the text, create cohesion, and clarify the relationships among complex ideas and concepts.	Use inappropriate transitions and syntax, or very few transitions, to link the major sections of the text, create cohesion, and clarify the relationships among complex ideas and concepts.

Figure B ǀ **Writing Rubric for Literary Analysis of Poetry** (*continued*)			
Advanced	**Proficient**	**Partially Proficient**	**Novice**
Use precise and highly effective language and literary terms to manage the complexity of the topic.	Use precise language and literary terms to manage the complexity of the topic.	Use simplistic language to describe the topic.	Use vague and unclear language to describe the topic.
Establish and maintain a sophisticated style and objective and knowledgeable tone.	Establish and maintain a formal style and objective tone.	Establish and maintain a formal style and objective tone through most of the essay.	Use an inconsistent style and tone.
Provide an insightful conclusion that follows from and supports the explanation presented.	Provide a conclusion that follows from and supports the explanation presented.	Provide a concluding summary of the explanation presented.	Provide a conclusion that is disconnected from the explanation presented.
Demonstrate strong command of the conventions of standard English grammar and usage when writing or speaking.	Demonstrate command of the conventions of standard English grammar and usage when writing or speaking.	Demonstrate some command of the conventions of standard English grammar and usage when writing or speaking.	Demonstrate very little command of the conventions of standard English grammar and usage when writing or speaking.

Exploring Theme, Purpose, and Rhetoric in the Declaration of Independence

Grade Level/Course: ELA grades 11–12
Length of Lesson: Two hours; two 60-minute class periods

Introduction

At the high school level, the Common Core State Standards for English Language Arts emphasize informational text reading and writing. Even though the Common Core includes literacy standards for history, science, and technical subjects, ELA teachers are now expected to teach several foundational American history documents and speeches, which is a departure from past practice.

It is not typical for standards documents to identify specific informational texts to be studied, but the Common Core document breaks from this convention and does name some American history documents that English language arts teachers will need to incorporate into lessons, including Washington's Farewell Address, the Gettysburg Address, King's "Letter from Birmingham Jail," the Bill of Rights, Supreme Court decisions, and the Declaration of Independence. In the lesson plan that follows, ELA standards from three strands—Reading (Informational Text), Speaking and Listening, and Writing—are woven together to guide a study of the Declaration of Independence.

Strategies from the Framework for Instructional Planning

- *Creating the Environment for Learning:* The essential question ("How is rhetoric used to promote themes and purpose in a text?") and learning objective ("To determine theme, purpose, and rhetoric in a document") are central to the lesson's content. The teacher provides feedback throughout the lesson, and students give feedback and recognition to one another for their effort and good ideas. Cooperative learning takes place as students work to comprehend the text through informal partnering and small groups. Cooperative learning is also built into Class #2, as students engage in a seminar discussion of the lesson's essential question.

- *Helping Students Develop Understanding:* The lesson incorporates several strategies to help students develop understanding. In Class #1, the teacher uses an advance organizer, a nonlinguistic representation (the oral recording of the document), and a graphic organizer for the homework assignment. In Class #2, the teacher gives the students a summarization writing assignment.

- *Helping Students Extend and Apply Knowledge:* The foundation skills developed in this lesson set the stage for future comparing and contrasting of the rhetoric in the Declaration of Independence with that in King George's response to the Americans.

Common Core State Standards—Knowledge and Skills to Be Addressed

Strand/Domain: Reading—Informational Text

Heading: Integration of Knowledge and Ideas

RI.11–12.9 Analyze seventeenth-, eighteenth-, and nineteenth-century foundational U.S. documents of historical and literary significance (including the Declaration of Independence, the Preamble to the Constitution, the Bill of Rights, and Lincoln's Second Inaugural Address) for their themes, purposes, and rhetorical features.

Strand: Writing

Heading: Text Types and Purposes

W.11–12.2b Write informative/explanatory texts to examine and convey complex ideas, concepts, and information clearly and accurately through the effective selection, organization, and analysis of content; develop the topic thoroughly by selecting the most significant and relevant facts, extended definitions, concrete details, quotations, or other information and examples appropriate to the audience's knowledge of the topic.

Strand: Speaking and Listening

Heading: Comprehension and Collaboration

SL.11–12.1 Initiate and participate effectively in a range of collaborative discussions (one-on-one, in groups, and teacher-led) with diverse partners on grades 11–12 topics, texts, and issues, building on others' ideas and expressing their own clearly and persuasively.

SL.11–12.3 Evaluate a speaker's point of view, reasoning, and use of evidence and rhetoric, assessing the stance, premises, links among ideas, word choice, points of emphasis, and tone used.

Common Core State Standards—Prior Knowledge and Skills to Be Applied

Strand/Domain: Reading—Informational Text

Heading: Key Ideas and Details

RI.11–12.1 Cite strong and thorough textual evidence to support analysis of what the text says explicitly as well as inferences drawn from the text, including determining where the text leaves matters uncertain.

Strand: Writing

Heading: Text Types and Purposes

W.11–12.2 Write informative/explanatory texts to examine and convey complex ideas, concepts, and information clearly and accurately through the effective selection, organization, and analysis of content.

Strand: Speaking and Listening

Heading: Comprehension and Collaboration

SL.11–12.1 Initiate and participate effectively in a range of collaborative discussions (one-on-one, in groups, and teacher-led) with diverse partners on grades 11–12 topics, texts, and issues, building on others' ideas and expressing their own clearly and persuasively.

Teacher's Lesson Summary

Through reading and discussion of the Declaration of Independence, students will explore the theme, purpose, and rhetoric found in the document and will write a summary that makes clear the relationships among theme, purpose, and rhetoric.

Essential Question: How is rhetoric used to promote themes and purpose in a text?
Learning Objective: To identify effective uses of theme, purpose, and rhetoric in a document and discuss these elements knowledgeably and effectively.

Knowledge/Vocabulary Objectives

At the conclusion of this lesson, students will

- Understand the rhetoric, theme, and purpose of key phrases and sentences in the document, such as the following:
  - ▸ "We hold these truths to be self-evident, that all men are created equal, that they are endowed by their Creator with certain unalienable Rights, that among these are Life, Liberty, and the pursuit of Happiness."
  - ▸ "That whenever any Form of Government becomes destructive of these ends, it is the Right of the People to alter or to abolish it. . . ."
  - ▸ "But when a long train of abuses and usurpations, pursuing invariably the same Object evinces a design to reduce them under absolute Despotism, it is their right, it is their duty, to throw off such Government, and to provide new Guards for their future security."
  - ▸ "The history of the present King of Great Britain is a history of repeated injuries and usurpations, all having in direct object the establishment of an absolute Tyranny over these States. To prove this, let Facts be submitted to a candid world."
  - ▸ ". . . a right inestimable to them and formidable to tyrants only."
  - ▸ ". . . for the sole purpose of fatiguing them into compliance with his measures."

> ▸ "... whereby the Legislative Powers, incapable of Annihilation, have returned to the People at large for their exercise. ..."
> ▸ "... swarms of Officers to harrass our People, and eat out their substance."
> ▸ "He has plundered our seas, ravaged our Coasts, burnt our towns, and destroyed the lives of our people."
> ▸ "... circumstances of Cruelty & perfidy scarcely paralleled in the most barbarous ages, and totally unworthy of the Head of a civilized nation."
> ▸ "A Prince whose character is thus marked by every act which may define a Tyrant, is unfit to be the ruler of a free People."

Skill/Process Objectives

At the conclusion of this lesson, students will be able to

- Identify rhetoric in a piece of writing.
- Knowledgably discuss and write about how rhetoric can support theme and purpose in a piece of writing.

Resources/Preparation Needed

- Copies of the Declaration of Independence, one per student. This document is easily obtained online
- An audio recording of the Declaration of Independence, also obtainable online
- A projectable three-column graphic organizer to model for students how to map the theme and purpose of specific pieces of rhetoric (see p. 96)
- An assessment tool students can use to guide their own discussion participation and inform peer assessment and feedback (see Figure A, p. 99), one per student

Activity Description to Share with Students

Rhetoric: What is it, and how did our Founding Fathers use it? In this lesson, you will explore the theme, purpose, and rhetoric of the Declaration of Independence by determining the meaning of key phrases and sentences and by engaging in a protocol-driven discussion after having read the document. In the discussion, you will explicitly refer to evidence from the text to stimulate a thoughtful, well-reasoned exchange of ideas about how the authors of the Declaration used rhetoric to promote purpose and theme. After the discussion, you will write a short essay summarizing your learning of how rhetoric was used to promote purpose and theme in the Declaration of Independence.

Lesson Activity Sequence—Class #1

Start the Lesson

1. Post and briefly discuss the essential question and learning objective.
2. Explain the term "rhetoric" in your own words and show the students an example of rhetoric from the Declaration of Independence.
3. Have students define "rhetoric" for themselves and ask them to come up with examples and nonexamples of what it is. Have them share these examples and nonexamples with a partner. Review several sets of examples and nonexamples as a whole class to make sure student understanding is on track, providing clarification as needed.

Engage Students in Learning the Content

1. As an advance organizer for the reading, direct students to create and fill out the first two columns of a KWL-style graphic organizer (see example) and discuss these responses with the same partner.

What I Know About Rhetoric in the Declaration of Independence	What I Want to Learn (or THINK I'll Learn) About Rhetoric in the Declaration of Independence	What I Learned About Rhetoric in the Declaration of Independence

2. Play a recording of the Declaration of Independence and ask students to read along silently, highlighting any phrases that they find confusing.

3. Ask students to work in collaborative learning groups of four to five and reread the Declaration orally among themselves. Tell them to pause as they read so that they may discuss and determine the meaning of the phrases they have questions about. Ask each group to identify and list rhetorical phrases to share with the rest of the class. (For a future lesson, students can explore how rhetoric also seems to be in the eye of the beholder; for example, they might contrast King George's take on these phrases with that of the revolutionaries.)

4. As the collaborative learning groups share the rhetorical phrases they found with the whole class, all students should mark these passages in their copies of the text. Be sure to give students feedback on their findings as they report out.

Close the Lesson

1. Have students write on their KWL advance organizer what they learned about the Declaration of Independence.

2. *Homework:* Ask students to reread the Declaration of Independence and make note of the rhetorical phrases that they want to link to the document's theme and purpose. They will need to create a three-column organizer with headings of *Rhetoric, Theme,* and *Purpose.* Show the following template as a model, and draw other examples from the rhetorical phrases listed on pages 93–94.

Rhetoric	Theme	Purpose
A Prince whose character is thus marked by every act which may define a Tyrant, is unfit to be the ruler of a free People.	Justification for not wanting the king as a leader.	To show the American people that the king is the wrong person to lead a new nation.

3. At the end of class, have students hand in their KWL advance organizers so that you can check for misunderstandings to address during the next class session.

Lesson Activity Sequence—Class #2

Start the Lesson

1. Ask a student to explain the learning objective and how it connects with the homework the class did.
2. Address misconceptions identified during your review of the previous day's advance organizers.
3. Preview the class session's discussion of rhetoric, theme, and purpose.

Engage Students in Learning the Content

1. In preparation for the discussion, check that students have completed the homework assignment, and allow them to discuss their graphic organizers with a partner. Tell them they may add new ideas to their organizers as these ideas come up in the discussion.
2. Review your discussion guidelines about the participant behaviors that support a good discussion. A suggestion: Set the class up in an inside-outside circle configuration, with half the class acting as the participants in the inside circle and the other half acting as peer discussion assessors in the outer circle. Use the guidelines you have set for discussions to create and distribute the **Discussion Participation Assessment Tool** (see **Figure A**, p. 99), a rubric that students can use to remind themselves of positive discussion behaviors and assess one another's performance.
3. Use the essential question as the discussion starter: "How is rhetoric used to promote themes and purpose in the Declaration of Independence?"
4. After 10–15 minutes, have the inside circle and outside circle switch places, and run the discussion again with the new participants.

Close the Lesson

1. Hold a "discussion debrief," using the time to clear up any misconceptions and to allow students to share their peer assessments with one other.
2. Review the learning objective and tie it to the homework assignment: to write a first-draft summary essay explaining how rhetoric serves the theme and purpose of the Declaration of Independence.

Additional Resources for This Lesson

- The full text of the Declaration of Independence is available for download at www.ushistory.org/declaration/document
- Available audio recordings of the Declaration of Independence include streaming audio from National Public Radio (www.npr.org/programs/morning/features/2002/jul/declaration/) and streaming and downloadable audio from Librivox (http://archive.org/details/declaration_of_independence_librivox).

Figure A	**Discussion Participation Assessment Tool**	
Characteristics of a Good Discussion Participant	**Comments on the Person You Assessed** (Provide Specific Examples)
Participant respects other participants. (Everyone's ideas are to be honored and respected.)	
Participant is an active listener; he or she builds on others' ideas by referring to them.	
Participant stays focused on the topic.	
Participant makes specific references to the text; he or she uses examples from the text to explain a point.	
Participant asks for clarification; he or she makes sure to understand the points that other participants are trying to make by asking questions.	

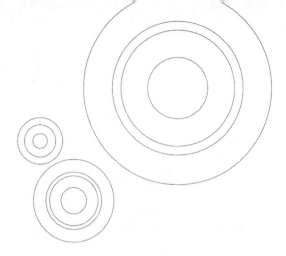

References

Coleman, D., & Pimentel, S. (2012). *Revised publishers' criteria for the Common Core State Standards in English language arts and literacy, grades 3–12*. Retrieved from http://www.corestandards.org/assets/Publishers_Criteria_for_3-12.pdf

Common Core State Standards Initiative. (2010a). *Application of Common Core State Standards for English language learners*. Washington, DC: CCSSO & National Governors Association. Retrieved from http://www.corestandards.org/assets/application-for-english-learners.pdf

Common Core State Standards Initiative. (2010b). *Application to students with disabilities*. Washington, DC: CCSSO & National Governors Association. Retrieved from http://www.corestandards.org/assets/application-to-students-with-disabilities.pdf

Common Core State Standards Initiative. (2010c). *Common Core State Standards for English language arts & literacy in history/social studies, science, and technical subjects*. Washington, DC: CCSSO & National Governors Association. Retrieved from http://www.corestandards.org/assets/CCSSI_ELA%20Standards.pdf

Common Core State Standards Initiative. (2010d). *Common Core State Standards for English language arts & literacy in history/social studies, science, and technical subjects. Appendix A: Research supporting key elements of the standards, glossary of key terms*. Washington, DC: CCSSO & National Governors Association. Retrieved from http://www.corestandards.org/assets/Appendix_A.pdf

Common Core State Standards Initiative. (2010e). *Common Core State Standards for English language arts & literacy in history/social studies, science, and technical subjects. Appendix B: Text exemplars and sample performance tasks*. Washington, DC: CCSSO & National Governors Association. Retrieved from http://www.corestandards.org/assets/Appendix_B.pdf

Common Core State Standards Initiative. (2010f). *Common Core State Standards for English language arts & literacy in history/social studies, science, and technical subjects. Appendix C: Samples of student writing.* Washington, DC: CCSSO & National Governors Association. Retrieved from http://www.corestandards.org/assets/Appendix_C.pdf

Dean, C. B., Hubbell, E. R., Pitler, H., & Stone, B. (2012). *Classroom instruction that works: Research-based strategies for increasing student achievement* (2nd ed.). Alexandria, VA: ASCD; and Boulder, CO: McREL.

Hess, K. (2011, December). *Learning progressions frameworks designed for use with the Common Core State Standards in English language arts & literacy K–12.* Retrieved from http://www.nciea.org/publication_PDFs/ELA_LPF_12%202011_final.pdf

Hess, K. (2012, January). *Content specifications with content mapping for the summative assessment of the Common Core State Standards for English language arts & literacy in history/social studies, science, and technical subject* [draft]. Retrieved from http://www.smarterbalanced.org/smarter-balanced-assessments/

Hess, K., & Hervey, S. (2011). *Tools for examining text complexity.* Retrieved from http://www.nciea.org/publication_PDFs/Updated%20toolkit-text%20complexity_KH12.pdf

Kansas State Department of Education. (2011). *Text complexity resources.* Retrieved from http://www.ksde.org/Default.aspx?tabid=4778#TextRes

Kendall, J. S. (2011). *Understanding Common Core State Standards.* Alexandria, VA: ASCD.

National Assessment Governing Board, U.S. Department of Education. (2011). *Writing framework for the 2011 National Assessment of Educational Progress.* Retrieved from http://www.eric.ed.gov/PDFS/ED512552.pdf

Nelson, J., Perfetti, C., Liben, D., & Liben, M. (2012). *Measures of text difficulty: Testing their predictive value for grade levels and student performance.* Retrieved from http://www.ccsso.org/Documents/2012/Measures%20ofText%20Difficulty_final.2012.pdf

Partnership for Assessment of Readiness for College and Careers. (2010). *Application for the Race to the Top comprehensive assessment systems competition.* Retrieved from http://www.parcconline.org/sites/parcc/files/PARCC%20Application%20-%20FINAL.pdf

Partnership for Assessment of Readiness for College and Careers. (2011, November). *PARCC model content frameworks: English language arts/literacy, grades 3–11.* Retrieved from http://www.parcconline.org/sites/parcc/files/PARCC%20MCF%20for%20ELA%20Literacy_Fall%202011%20Release%20%28rev%29.pdf

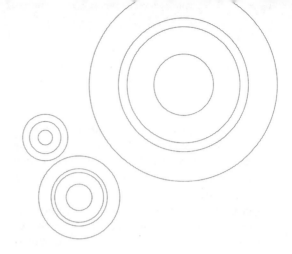

About the Authors

Susan Ryan is a consultant at Mid-continent Research for Education and Learning (McREL). She has reviewed, revised, and developed language arts standards documents for many districts, state agencies, and education organizations. Ms. Ryan has conducted alignment reviews on assessment items, instructional materials, and curriculum materials. Her work with the Common Core State Standards includes the production of gap analyses, crosswalks, transition documents, alignment reviews, and research support for state departments of education. Ms. Ryan has also facilitated teacher leaders in curriculum development and implementation of the Common Core. She was a consulting state content expert for English language arts during the development of the Common Core and a state consultant to the Partnership for Assessment of Readiness for College and Careers (PARCC) consortium. A former high school language arts teacher, she holds a BA in English from the University of Colorado and a secondary teaching license through Metropolitan State University of Denver.

 **Dana Frazee** is a principal consultant at McREL. She conducts workshops and training on curriculum and system improvement. She works with districts and teachers in North Dakota and Wyoming on the implementation of the Common Core English Language Arts standards. Ms. Frazee has been a middle school and high school teacher, a teacher leader, the principal of a K–8 charter school, and a K–12 educational consultant. She has facilitated numerous regional and national workshops on a variety of subjects, including data-based decision making, writing in the content area, formative assessment, continuous school improvement, and effective instructional strategies. Ms. Frazee coauthored *Teaching Reading in the Content Area*, 3rd edition (2012) and McREL's *Math in Afterschool: An Instructor's Guide to the Afterschool Training Toolkit* (2008). She earned her bachelor's degree from the University of Colorado at Boulder and her master's degree from Adams State College, Colorado.

John Kendall (Series Editor) is Senior Director in Research at McREL in Denver. Having joined McREL in 1988, Mr. Kendall conducts research and development activities related to academic standards. He directs a technical assistance unit that provides standards-related services to schools, districts, states, and national and international organizations. He is the author of *Understanding Common Core State Standards, the* senior author of *Content Knowledge: A Compendium of Standards and Benchmarks for K–12 Education*, and the author or coauthor of numerous reports and guides related to standards-based systems. These works include *High School Standards and Expectations for College and the Workplace, Essential Knowledge: The Debate over What American Students Should Know,* and *Finding the Time to Learn: A Guide*. He holds an MA in Classics and a BA in English Language and Literature from the University of Colorado at Boulder.

About McREL

Mid-continent Research for Education and Learning (McREL) is a nationally recognized nonprofit education research and development organization headquartered in Denver, Colorado, with offices in Honolulu, Hawaii, and Omaha, Nebraska. Since 1966, McREL has helped translate research and professional wisdom about what works in education into practical guidance for educators. Our more than 120 staff members and affiliates include respected researchers, experienced consultants, and published writers who provide educators with research-based guidance, consultation, and professional development for improving student outcomes.

ASCD and Common Core State Standards Resources

ASCD believes that for the Common Core State Standards to have maximum effect, they need to be part of a well-rounded, whole child approach to education that ensures students are healthy, safe, engaged, supported, and challenged.

For a complete and updated overview of ASCD's resources related to the Common Core standards, including other *Quick-Start Guides* in the Understanding the Common Core State Standards series, professional development institutes, online courses, links to webinars and to ASCD's free EduCore™ digital tool, and lots more, please visit us at **www.ascd.org/commoncore.**